WHICH NONE
CAN SHUT

WHICH NONE
CAN SHUT

REMARKABLE TRUE STORIES OF GOD'S
MIRACULOUS WORK IN THE MUSLIM WORLD

✦

REEMA GOODE

TYNDALE™
MOMENTUM

An Imprint of
Tyndale House Publishers, Inc.

Visit Tyndale online at www.tyndale.com.

Visit Tyndale Momentum online at www.tyndalemomentum.com.

TYNDALE is a registered trademark of Tyndale House Publishers, Inc. *Tyndale Momentum* and the Tyndale Momentum logo are trademarks of Tyndale House Publishers, Inc. Tyndale Momentum is an imprint of Tyndale House Publishers, Inc.

Which None Can Shut: Remarkable True Stories of God's Miraculous Work in the Muslim World

ISBN 978-1-4143-3720-3

Printed in the United States of America

19 18 17 16 15 14 13
11 10 9   8   7   6   5

To GOD

*Oh, that men would give thanks to the L*ORD *for His goodness,*
And for His wonderful works to the children of men!

PSALM 107:8

Contents

Foreword

We need to hear stories.

Jesus told stories.

I tell stories.

There is no substitute for stories because each one includes echoes from your story, or mine, or that of our children.

The nomad in the desert, the kite flyer in Kabul, the street kid in New York, the terrorist on the mountains in Pakistan, the stone thrower in Gaza or Bethlehem—every one of them has a story, and it needs to be told.

Why? Because Jesus died for and still loves every one of them. Their stories help us connect them to the redeeming power of Jesus so we can love and pray for them until each of them, too, is transformed into a positive force to make the world a better place.

Why is it that we see their stories as so different from ours?

They were all born as innocent babies, not as terrorists.

Many were born in countries where the message of God's love was not known. Does that mean they should not have a chance to hear it?

Why is it we have not yet spread the Good News among them?

Maybe we heard God's call but did not go . . . did not tell, did not share, did not care . . .

Maybe we thought it was too dangerous. But not caring and sharing is far more dangerous!

Yes, each person has a story; in fact, this book is full of them. What these stories from the Arabian Peninsula tell us is what happens when they meet the love of Jesus.

And that is why I look forward to a hundred more books like this one. It's not just "their" story; it is "His" story.

— *Brother Andrew*

Acknowledgments

My husband, Mike, and I would like to acknowledge the many people who helped make this book, and even the stories in it, possible. Although we cannot mention names for reasons of privacy and safety, we want to publicly express our gratitude to the Body of Christ.

Thanks to our coworkers on the field. You all have stories like these, and we hope that this book well represents our mutual experience here in the Arabian Peninsula. Thanks to our dearly beloved teammates, who prayed and worked with us as these stories and events actually unfolded. Thanks to the quiet gentleman who first took an interest in bringing our stories to the public and planted the seed of faith that made me think I might actually write a book one day. Thanks to the dear couple who undergirded us with their prayerful support, inspiring us to believe God for great things.

Thanks to the servant leaders who saw the potential of the book. They connected us to others in the Body of Christ who are capable of doing what we aren't and have held our hand through the entire process. Thanks to our field leadership who, on more than one occasion, allowed us the freedom to do what we felt God was leading us to do, even when it went a bit against the normal grain. Thanks to the many, many believers around the world whose enduring prayers and financial sacrifices have provided the power for all our lights to shine in this darkness. The Lord's richest blessings upon each one of you. You know who you are, and so does He.

The Story behind the Storyteller

MEET REEMA GOODE

As a little girl, Reema remembers being very affected by Cecil B. DeMille's film *The Ten Commandments*. She believed in God and prayed to Him every night, even as a young adult. Still, she did not learn how to begin a personal relationship with God and find forgiveness for her sins until her early twenties, when she read a little Christian booklet someone had left lying around at work. It was the first explanation of the Gospel that Reema had ever understood. Immediately she gave her life to Christ and couldn't wait to tell others about Him.

Her first attempts to share the Good News probably confused people more than helped them. What were you supposed to say? How were you supposed to say it? Clearly not gifted to "preach," Reema decided to think through what had happened to her and start by telling people that. As it turned out, many people could relate to her story and wanted to know more about a God who was so real and involved in ordinary people's lives.

In an effort to meet other Christians, Reema went to a different church every Sunday she had off from work for an entire year. But when she asked about their faith, people would talk about when they'd begun attending services or how they'd become church members, deacons, or Sunday school teachers. None of them seemed to know what she meant by "having a personal relationship with God" or "deciding to follow Christ." Reema realized that, like her, many people grew up believing they were Christians simply because they belonged to a denomination or went to meetings. But then, she wondered, where were all the Christians? Why were they so hard for her to find?

Tuning in to the radio one day, she heard a program that seemed to give her the answer. It was Moody Bible Institute's *Stories of Great Christians*, the dramatized testimonies of famous missionaries. Hearing how believers had left the comforts of home to bring the Gospel to the ends of the earth made Reema wonder: Had all the Christians already gone to other countries where the message of the Bible was unknown, unavailable, or even banned? Her humorous naiveté served to draw her on to more serious thoughts.

The revelation that there were still places in the world where people could live their entire lives and die without ever having heard the Gospel caused Reema to ask herself a question. With what she now knew, how could she stay in America, where there were Bibles in every bookstore and complete freedom to choose Christ? And so, although she finally did find other followers of Christ and became an active part of a church fellowship, Reema was now committed to going to an unevangelized field someday. It turned out she wouldn't be going alone.

Reema met Mike in a cafeteria. She happened to get in line next to him, and then he followed her to her seat and wouldn't go away. She was actually a little miffed, assuming that this obviously older man, who was also tall and handsome, must be married. It soon became clear he was not. He was a single Christian man who had committed himself to serving God on an unevangelized field, and he was looking for a like-minded wife to go with him. They were married within the year.

While Mike finished his final two years of Bible college, Reema wrote to a number of agencies asking for information that might help them narrow their missionary direction to a specific place or people group. Where were the most people who were the least reached? Before beginning their search, Mike and Reema had barely heard anything about Islam.

Half anticipating that they would end up working with a remote jungle tribe, they were surprised when the Lord began to lay the Arab Muslim World on their hearts. But the more they learned about it, the more that burden grew.

After three years of establishing a church support base to stand behind them, Mike and Reema arrived on the Arabian Peninsula. They, along with their two children, Tim and Lydia, are still there.

Preface

God works in mysterious ways, and sometimes through seemingly unrelated events.

In 1990, Luis Bush coined the term "the 10/40 Window," referring to an area of the globe that is home to the largest, most unreached people groups on the planet. Also in 1990, U.S. president George H. W. Bush initiated a military action in the Persian Gulf, known as Operation Desert Storm. These two unrelated events had a profound effect on the Body of Christ. How? God used both of them to draw the eyes of His Church onto the Muslim World— a world whose population, at that time, claimed one-fifth of humanity and had virtually no Gospel witness. Over the next two decades, a succession of world events sharpened the focus of attention even further—onto not only the Muslim World at large, but the Arab Muslim World in particular.

Words that never touched our lives before became part of our everyday vocabulary: *Quran, Allah, burqa, jihad.* Awareness and concern for the one billion people living under Islamic rule skyrocketed. Books on Islam, Arab culture, and how to share your faith with a Muslim came out in droves. Multitudes of Christians around the world began to pray, give, and go.

Now after two decades of concerted and growing effort by the Church, the televised news from the Middle East seems to be just as depressing as ever. Is God answering our prayers? Is He actually doing anything in the lives of Muslims? If so, what? That's what this book is all about.

Our family has been living in the midst of a typical Muslim neighborhood, in Arabia, for more than a dozen years. We want to let you see what we get to see as Christians living "on the ground" inside an Islamic country. We believe you will be greatly encouraged.

We want to let you see what we get to see as Christians living "on the ground" inside an Islamic country.

This is not a book about the religion of Islam itself or about Arab culture, nor is it a book about how to minister to Muslims, as there are many excellent volumes already written on those subjects. We'd like to shift the vantage point, refocusing the reader's lens from a distant "aerial view" of the Muslim World at large to "zoom in" on how God has actually been working in the practical, everyday life of just one of many Islamic communities over the past several years. Instead of sharing statistics about how Muslims are coming to Christ, we want to walk you through the local scenery where we live through stories, and let you see for yourself the incredibly creative, diverse, unexpected, and thrilling ways in which God is reaching our neighbors with the Gospel of Jesus Christ. His Word is spreading, and His Spirit is confirming the Truth to their hearts in very real ways.

Although the stories in this book are encouraging, uplifting, and sometimes even humorous, we do not deny that the Muslim World is often a dangerous place. Where we live, leading a local to Christ is a punishable crime. Muslims who convert know they will probably suffer persecution or even death. Nevertheless, every year more Christians come to live as witnesses for Christ in Arabia, and every year reports of stories like these are increasing in number and frequency.

The following accounts are all real-life events happening in real time to people we know personally. Of course some of the details, and all the names of people and places, have been changed in order to protect those involved.

It's our prayer that *Which None Can Shut* will glorify God, inspire His people in their own walks of faith, and encourage believers everywhere that God's loving Light is penetrating the Dark Fortress. We also hope these stories will ignite more prayer for the Muslim World, and more compassion for those living under its rule, as they demonstrate how God is opening doors for the Gospel, confirming His Word, revealing His love, and winning hearts in Arabia.

Yes! God *is* answering prayer and He *is* building His Church! If the gates of Hell won't prevail against it, how can Islam?

✛

See, I have set before you an open door,
and no one can shut it.

REVELATION 3:8

CHAPTER 1

The Open Door

It was a winter night in Little Town, Arabia. The crisp evening breeze was a welcome change from summer's daytime highs of 120-plus degrees. As I shuffled through the irregular and unpaved hardpan streets, the warmly spiced smells of *asha*, the evening meal, arose from every house to comfort the chilly air outside. It was after nine o'clock, and as the women washed up the dishes, children who normally came out to play for a couple of hours before bedtime had opted to snuggle up in sweaters and caps indoors, in front of their televisions where it was warmer. The empty stillness of the well-worn streets amplified the quiet padding of my sandals on the dirt. A lack of streetlamps made the glittering stars above all the more vivid against the black sky. And that moon! A huge crescent, the very symbol of Islam, seemed to be hanging directly above our village like a signboard, a symbol of ownership. Joy bubbled up in my heart as I contemplated where I was and what I was doing. Here, beneath the dominating rule of the Crescent, I was on my way to a Bible and Quran discussion with neighborhood women.

"Come . . . and bring the books!" they had said. But even more amazing was that they had said it often. Within eighteen months of arriving, our family had been able to share the Gospel at least once with virtually all of our neighborhood friends, and God was confirming His Word to be true in their individual lives. It was incredible the way He opened doors, and it had all started in a quite unexpected way through a rather ordinary event.

Within eighteen months of arriving, our family had been able to share the Gospel at least once with virtually all of our neighborhood friends.

We had just moved into the neighborhood and hadn't put much effort into meeting the neighbors yet, as we needed some time to adjust to simply "living" first. There was no city water, so the tank on the roof had to be refilled by water truck every five or six days. Every morning we filtered our drinking water and put it in the refrigerator to cool. The fridge wasn't coping well with the desert heat, so we purchased only a little food at a time to avoid its spoiling.

In those first weeks, it seemed like nothing worked the way it was supposed to, or at least not the way we were used to. The oven had no mechanism for telling temperature; it was simply "on" or "off," which suddenly made cooking a new challenge. Our first load of laundry had been torn to shreds by the washer, limiting our limited wardrobe even further. We had not been able to flush the toilet for two days, and floor drains in the kitchen and bathrooms were plugged with trash, toys, and rags from previous tenants. Knowing that hospitality is such an important part of Arab culture, it seemed there was little point in meeting the neighbors until we had a decent place to invite them to. After initial greetings and small talk, it is polite to say "*Taali bayti*" ["Come to my house"], and we wanted to be ready for them to take us up on that offer. However, there was another reason we hadn't met the neighbors yet, which we wouldn't find out about until later.

Apparently, the *mutawwa*s had warned the local people about us. Being religious teachers who provide guidance and spiritual assistance, they told their flocks that foreigners who come to work in Arabia are Christian missionaries sent to deceive their children, bring in immorality, destroy their families and country, and corrupt Islamic society as a whole. Of course, it's true that we were (and are) Christian missionaries, but our motives could not have been more opposite that description. This erroneous preconception was to become the first hurdle that God overcame for us.

Before coming to Little Town, my husband, Mike, and I had had to fulfill some specific requirements of our mission board, in addition to regular Bible training, to prepare for work in the Muslim World. We read books on Islam and cross-cultural issues, and Mike got some very practical experience reaching out to a Muslim population within the United States. The history of missions to Muslims overall seemed pretty discouraging then. In the past, Christian workers had sacrificed so much; they had labored so long and so hard over years and even lifetimes, with seemingly little fruit. In those days, the evangelical Church in general had little knowledge of the Muslim World. There were very few workers and little prayer support.

We believe our experience in Arabia is a direct result of the dramatic increase in intercessory prayer for Muslims and missionaries to Muslims.

However in the 1990s, through the emerging focus on the 10/40 Window and the headlines generated by Operation Desert Storm, all that changed. The face of the worldwide Church turned to look upon the unreached masses of humanity living under Islamic rule. Multitudes of Christians around the world began to pray, and things started to happen. Followers of Christ began to find ways to become residents in Muslim countries where missionary activity is banned by law and constitutes a punishable crime. God began to open doors that were previously shut tight. We believe that our experience in Arabia is a direct result of the dramatic increase in intercessory prayer being made for Muslims and missionaries to Muslims by the Church around the world. For us, the door to our neighborhood began to crack open in a very unexpected way, through the humble means of a car that wouldn't start.

One morning as I was getting our three-year-old son, Tim, ready for the day, my husband, Mike, and I noticed the sound of a car engine outside turning over and over without catching. Being a "motor head" from his youth, Mike naturally went out to see what was going on.

He stepped outside our concrete block house into the gravel yard and a warm, sunny winter's day. A few more steps and he was through the metal gate that permitted entrance to our yard through a seven-foot-high wall. All the concrete houses had concrete walls surrounding them, giving privacy to women who had to emerge from homes to hang wash or go to kitchens, which were usually not attached to the rest of the house.

Since cooking smells in the home were considered unpleasant, incense was burned in all the living quarters to give a fragrant, welcoming smell. Mike could smell the after-breakfast incense in the air as he came out into the dirt road.

There were homes in all directions, with no apparent order or municipal plan. Some of the streets were barely wide enough to drive through; others could accommodate five cars parked side by side. In fact, when visitors came to any particular house, there often were several cars parked that way in the street at once, blocking it completely.

On a weekday morning like this, however, few vehicles were around, since the children had been taken to school and the men had left for work. One car remained, hood open, under a scraggly thorn tree. A small group of men had gathered in front of it. Wearing their freshly pressed robes and traditional head coverings, they surveyed the situation under the hood with their hands folded neatly behind them. It was obvious no one knew what to do, but they were supporting their neighbor by standing by him in his trouble.

As Mike approached, he shouted a cheery greeting, "*Salaam alaykum!*" The men looked up and responded tentatively, "*Alaykum assalaam.*" Then Mike stepped right into their midst to assess the situation. It was a simple matter of cleaning and setting the points. A few minutes later, he motioned for the gentleman to start his engine. It caught immediately. A look of amazed appreciation came over the men, and they lifted their hands in the air in that time-honored thumbs-up gesture that any Westerner would be sure to understand. Someone who knew a bit of English patted him on the back and exclaimed, "Number one! Number one!" The next thing Mike knew, he had been invited to several houses for coffee to reciprocate the favor. Later we would learn that this was not an initial gesture of friendship, but a traditional means of erasing indebtedness. Nevertheless, our family now had the opportunity to meet the neighbors.

At each home, Mike was invited into the men's *majlis*, a special room reserved for receiving visitors. Women and children were ushered into separate quarters, and all of us were lavished with fine Arab hospitality. First we were brought cold water and juices, then dates and coffee, then an assortment of delicious foods, all skillfully prepared by the women of the house. We felt welcome indeed! However, it soon became apparent to our hosts that something was wrong with us. We didn't seem to know how to eat normally.

To start with, we had some trouble just getting our bodies down onto the floor where the meal was being served. This being our first visit to each neighbor's home, we exerted every effort to follow all of the cultural rules we had been taught. *Don't let your backside point at anyone when you bend over.* Hard to do, when getting onto the floor in a room full of people. *Never ask someone to serve you by passing food, and eat only with your right hand.* Okay, I'd have to get my right side within an arm's length of that tray, without bumping or shoving any of the other eight people who were drawing tightly together around the *fou'alla* to eat. *Don't show anyone the sole of your foot.* Shoeless and surrounded on the floor, there didn't seem to be any possible physical position left to sit in without breaking some kind of rule. Or some part of my body. I began to wonder why yoga wasn't included in our missionary training. Our contorted efforts were, shall we say, less than graceful.

Once in position, and trying to ignore the pain of our legs falling asleep under us, we turned our minds to the task of actually eating. Our hosts sat on the floor and ate everything, including grains of rice and slippery noodles, very neatly and effortlessly without the aid of plates, forks, or spoons. Even women wearing face coverings managed to enjoy their meal without getting a drop on themselves. We, on the other hand, appeared to have never eaten before. How pathetic we must have looked with food all down our fronts and in our laps. I think I may have gotten some on the lady sitting next to me. How would our Muslim neighbors ever listen to a message shared by grown adults who couldn't even feed themselves with their own hands?

My family is living testimony to the fact that God can use anybody. As embarrassing as it was to be counted "clueless" in our new community, it disarmed the fear they had of us. Our very ineptitude was what gently opened the door to their hearts. We became the neighborhood project. Someone had to help this helpless American family.

As far as the *mutawwas'* warnings were concerned, if this was the best that the Christians could send to destroy Islamic society as they knew it, there was certainly nothing to fear.

As embarrassing as it was to be counted "clueless" in our new community, it disarmed the fear our neighbors had of us.

Our neighbors took us under their wings and began to instruct us for our betterment, not only in dining technique but in other areas as well. They taught me how to make proper coffee and how to cook traditional dishes. (I think that was partly to help me and partly so they could enjoy "decent food" when they came to our house, which they did often.) The men explained to Mike how haggling works so he could avoid overpaying too much in the markets. (As a white Westerner, he'd still be overcharged—but not so much as an ignorant white Westerner.) The women showed me how to wrap my veil so it would stop falling off. They let us know how we should handle various social situations, answered our many questions, and gave us advice.

For our part, we offered what we had to them. Mike

helped men with car and household repair questions (and was saved from becoming the neighborhood mechanic by the fact that all his tools were in America). He trimmed the trees so everyone could park their cars under them, out of the blistering sun. We helped kids who came to us with questions about their English homework. Our son, Tim, was more than happy to have a few dozen playmates sharing his swing and his toys. Being the only woman in our neighborhood with a driver's license, I could take the ladies to the *souq* (market) or the hospital, or to visit a friend who lived beyond walking distance. In short, we became *friends*.

Being friends with an Arab means visiting. They visit you. You visit them. If you can't go visit, you call and visit on the phone. There are even specific times of day for visiting various people. In Little Town, the ladies would visit each other in the morning at an appointed time between doing the chores and cooking the main midday meal. Men would visit men and families would visit families in the evening between the last two prayer calls of the day. To visit others was to honor them because you had made the trip to come and see them. They, in turn, honored you with hospitality. For us, visiting became the core of our ministry.

God had built a wide-open door of opportunity right into the culture, and we simply walked through it.

I mean, what do you actually do on a visit? (Besides eat.) You sit and listen. You get to know people. You talk! Talking with our neighbors was exactly what we wanted to do, and now we were expected to do it regularly. God had built a wide-open door of opportunity right into the culture, and we simply walked through it.

Amidst all the discussions about schools, inflation, weddings, cooking, politics, health care, and the rest, we had numberless conversations about spiritual things. It was our privilege to be the first Christians most of our Arab Muslim neighbors had ever met, and we wanted to make the absolute most of it. During that first term, we learned all we could about what our friends believed and why. They, in turn, wanted to know about us. We shared the Gospel at every opportunity, and there were many opportunities. Muslims even shared the Gospel with each other. One woman took a copy of the *JESUS* film from us and invited a bunch of friends over to watch it with her in her *majlis*. Another took an audiocassette series of the dramatized Bible and listened to it with her morning visit group. Who would have dreamed it would be like this?

Once, a fellow Christian worker gave us an Arabic paper that was circulating on the Internet titled "What the Quran Says about the Bible and Jesus." It was intended to stir

Muslims' interest in the Bible. Being novices in the language, we gave it to our friend Habiiba and asked her to let us know if it said anything interesting—and if what it said was true. Apparently the answer to both questions was yes, because she took it to the local religious teacher for an explanation.

In her very own Quran, she'd confirmed that Sura 6:114-115 says the Bible is God's Word, which "was sent down from the Lord in truth"; that it should not be doubted; and that no one can change it. Yet every Muslim is taught to believe that the Bible has been changed and corrupted. Why? Well, from our viewpoint it's because Muhammad himself thought that his teachings were in agreement with the Bible. At least, with what he had heard of it, since he was illiterate himself. And how many of his followers back in the sixth century had Bibles to compare doctrine with? It wasn't until enough people could acquire books and read them for themselves that the conflicting natures of the Holy Scriptures and the Quran needed to be explained. Hence, the eruption of the teaching among Muslims that the Bible had been falsified somewhere in history—even though such a statement denies the very teaching of the Quran itself.

Such falsehoods persist largely because of ignorance. Indeed, if we had looked up these verses ourselves, we probably would have missed the issue altogether, because most

English translations of the Quran have since been "modified" to eliminate the dilemma such verses pose. But Habiiba was an Arab reading the Arabic text, and she knew there was no mistaking what it said. In all the times she had read the Quran, how could she have missed this? There were other problems brought up by the paper as well, and she decided to take them to the local mosque and ask for guidance. There had to be an explanation.

A devout Muslim, Habiiba was a credit to her well-respected family and proud of her heritage. She had no doubt that the religious teacher had a simple answer for all of this. But instead he became angry at her. He tore up the pages in front of her, and then told her to go home and forget everything she'd read. "Good Muslims don't read such trash," he'd said. She was appalled at his reaction and his treatment of her. She was a good Muslim. It was her wholehearted faith in Islam that had brought her to him for help. She was also intelligent and realized his overreaction meant he had no solution to the problem. This had a profound affect on Habiiba.

In recounting the experience, she determinedly told us, "I will never forget what was written in those papers!" Rather than squelching her interest, her zeal to validate her Islamic faith increased. Habiiba and two of her sisters became my best friends in the neighborhood. It was they who started the practice of calling me late at night to "bring the books." Although their motive was to explain and confirm the truth of Islam rather than to investigate Christianity, they were as eager to listen as they were to speak.

In their efforts to vindicate their religion, my friends were inadvertently exploring the basis for their own personal faith. What do Muslims believe? Exactly why do they believe it? Were they simply following the natural course of conformity to family and societal belief systems, or was there compelling evidence for Islam? As for me, whenever I shared a verse, I had them read it out loud to each other directly from the Arabic Bible. This not only saved time and prevented me from butchering the text, but it allowed them to see God's Word for themselves. I peppered the teaching with personal illustrations of how God and His Word were working in my own life and the lives of our family and friends. The freedom to share was amazing. We found virtually all of our neighbors were open to some depth of spiritual conversation.

This openness God had created wasn't limited to our neighborhood either. One morning I was looking for kitchen gadgets at a little shop run by an Iranian Muslim. He quickly helped me with my order and nervously asked, "Are you a

Christian?" I'd barely answered before he blurted out the rest of his question. "Can you get me a Bible?"

One day, Mike got into a taxi and the driver asked him, "Are you a Christian?" (This is not the way most conversations start off in the Muslim World!) It turned out that the cabdriver was an Arab who had been born in Jerusalem. As a young man, he had become a Jew. After some time, he concluded that Judaism wasn't "it" and joined the Orthodox Christian Church. Later he rejected "Christianity" and became a Muslim. Finally, being disillusioned with them all, he had decided to bypass religion altogether and "go direct" to God. But how? After arriving at his destination, Mike stayed in the cab another forty-five minutes to explain exactly how to "go direct." Afterwards the driver said, "If that's the way it is, I like it! Thank you for opening my eyes to this!"

A more recent story also dramatizes what God is doing in Muslim hearts today. I was Christmas shopping at one of the many bargain centers in Big Town, another city some distance from our home. While I was going through the checkout, the young Muslim cashier made a mistake and undercharged me. Although he hadn't noticed, I pointed it out to him for the sake of my own integrity. At first he smiled as if to say, "How dumb can you get?" But then his face softened and grew thoughtful, and he thanked me.

"No problem," I cheerily responded, not even attempting to witness or share a verse with him in front of all the other Muslim employees. My white, foreign face told them that I was probably a "Christian"—not to mention that I had just bought several rolls of cheap Chinese Christmas wrapping paper. As I was loading the bags into the car a minute later, I realized I was thirsty and made a mental note to buy water at BigMart, my next stop. But the Holy Spirit seemed to interrupt my thinking: *Go back in and buy it here.* My first thought was, *Why? You don't like BigMart?* Still, I locked up the car and obediently went back in to get the water.

As I approached the register with my bottle in hand, two Muslim men wearing prayer caps to signify their piety stepped in front of me and dropped their armloads of goods down on the checkout counter. I had only a single item! The American part of me wanted to shout, "I was born in freedom! You can't cut in front of me!" The Christian part of me was thinking, *How can I turn this into an opportunity to show God's love?* Reasoning that no one can take anything away from me that I freely give them, I forfeited my "rights" with a cheery "*Tfaddalu*"—politely offering to let them go ahead of me. (*Love is not proud . . . love is patient . . . love seeks not its own,* I reminded myself.) The men responded with a derisive look that seemed to say, "Honey, we're going ahead of you whether you say *tfaddalu* or not."

Although they had been completely unaffected by my attempt at grace, God did have a reason for all this. Waiting for them to check out meant it took longer for me to leave the store, and that is what gave the young Muslim cashier, whom I'd checked out with before, time to ask for his break, go outside, and walk down the street. By the time I finally paid for the water, got in the car, and began to drive away, that young man was waiting for me. Safely out of view from fellow Muslims, he waved me down. I pulled over and rolled down the window. "Can I help you?"

His words caught me completely off guard. "Yes, miss. I am a Muslim, but I want to become a Christian. Can you tell me how?"

Safely out of view from fellow Muslims, he waved me down. "I am a Muslim, but I want to become a Christian. Can you tell me how?"

When I introduced him to Mike later, young Ahmad explained what was in his heart. "I am a Muslim, and I know that we Muslims are not straight. We're crooked. But all of the Christians I know, they are like your wife. They are all straight. I want to be a Christian."

These stories, like hundreds of others, testify that this harvest field is no longer the barren granite of yesteryear. God has broken up the fallow ground and prepared the soil. The prayers of His worldwide Church have plowed it. The sweat and tears of generations of faithful witnesses have watered it. The cooperative efforts of the Body of Christ across centuries and around the globe have sown it. The prayer warriors, missionaries, tentmakers, translators, producers of outreach materials and media, broadcasters of Christian programming, as well as those who spread the light through their businesses, Web sites, chat rooms, sports outreaches, and a host of other means are all being used toward the burgeoning harvest. All are part of a picture that is too big to see from any single vantage point. And so it should be, that the glory for the harvest will be no one's but His.

✢

Finally, brethren, pray for us,
that the word of the Lord may run
swiftly and be glorified . . . and that we
may be delivered from unreasonable and
wicked men; for not all have faith.

2 THESSALONIANS 3:1-2

CHAPTER 2

Dealing with the Fear

It had sounded like any normal phone call. Any normal invitation. "Come over Thursday at nine," Mozi had said. Mike would be home to watch the kids by that time, so it was okay with him. We suspected nothing.

We had become part of the neighborhood furniture in those first few years. Spending time in each other's homes was routine. Mozi had often invited me over late, and so did other women. After the day's work was done, the last set of prayers was over, and dinner was cleaned up, the women had some time to themselves. Earlier, during "regular" visiting hours, there might be several guests at the same time, and it would be difficult to have any meaningful conversation. But after nine all was quiet. Sometimes we'd talk for hours, often about spiritual things.

Mozi and the seven other female relatives who shared her
home had become especially close to me. We'd spent count-
less hours together visiting, talking,
and just living life. Mike and I were so
trusted by the family that we had been
permitted to drive some of the ladies to
Third City, two hours away, and break
the Ramadan fast together at their
relatives' home. On another occasion,
I had had the distinct honor of taking
a gaggle of them out for their first dinner at a restaurant
with no male escort at all! They had been as excited as high
schoolers on prom night. Hilma, completely veiled except for
her eyes, kept peeking over her menu at the mixed crowd all
around her. I knew these women and they knew me. I loved
them. When Mozi called that night, there was no reason at
all to suspect that it was a setup.

*When Mozi called
that night, there
was no reason at
all to suspect that
it was a setup.*

Perhaps if we had known more about the male relatives of
the family, we would have been suspicious. But in God's sovereignty, Mike had developed his relationships with other men
in the neighborhood. Despite my frequent visits, I didn't know
the male relatives who lived in the house either, just because it
was considered indiscreet to ask about them. After all, as the
cultural reasoning went, why would a woman be interested in
another family's men? But those men knew about me.

It wasn't really me or my family that was the problem, though. It was God. As the Good News spread, God had been confirming the Truth in various ways to various people. When He answered a prayer for two members of their own household in dramatic fashion, Mozi's menfolk weren't grateful, they were upset.

Two of Mozi's sisters had had the *jinn* inside them, and nothing Islam had to offer was able to get those demons out. For three months, the family had taken the girls to various *mutawwa*s for treatment. These men are considered religious experts, and they offer spiritual counsel to their fellow Muslims—for a price. The girls were subjected to the potions and "treatments" of seven different *mutawwa*s, at the cost of a small fortune, but nothing helped. Although the whole story is contained in chapter 6, suffice it to say here that the girls were finally freed from the *jinn* by one prayer in Jesus' name. It was like Mount Carmel, the contest between the God of Elijah and the prophets of Baal. As Elijah said, "You call on the name of your gods, and I will call on the name of the LORD; and the God who answers . . . He is God" (1 Kings 18:24). When God answered the Christians' prayer and delivered the girls, it shook the core of this family's world.

Just like in the days when Jesus walked the earth, His works divided people. Some believed and were drawn toward

Him; others became angry and lashed out at Him. One of the men in Mozi's household who decided to lash out happened to work for the Special Intelligence Agency (SIA). The secret police.

Thursday night came. We finished our dinner and did the usual bedtime routine as a family. By this time our second child, three-year-old Lydia, was old enough to pray with us before I left for the appointment. It was our custom to pray for each other whenever we went out on an opportunity to share Christ.

Just like in the days when Jesus walked the earth, His works divided people. Some believed and were drawn toward Him; others became angry and lashed out at Him.

I arrived at Mozi's house on the opposite end of Little Town shortly after nine. Strangely, it was very quiet. Usually when I came to visit, there were at least the sounds of TVs inside, some kids bustling around the yard, and a few of the ladies coming to the gate to welcome me in. This evening only Jamila, the ancient-looking bedouin grandmother, appeared to greet me. Despite her years, Jamila was a firecracker of quick wit and hearty laughter. Her bright, chatty personality was subdued now, and she kept looking at the ground instead of at my face. When she apologized that Mozi and the others were not home, I assured her I was happy to be in her company. "No problem! You can tell me some of those great stories from the old days," I suggested. We went into the women's *majlis* and sat down on the carpet. Instead of sitting face-to-face, Jamila sat beside me, facing the door. That seemed odd, but I still did not suspect anything. Two minutes later, the door blew open.

A man burst into the room. A man. In the women's *majlis*. Alarm bells went off in my head. *This doesn't happen. Something's wrong.* The man was clearly angry. Volcanic angry. His fists were clenched, and his chest was heaving. The look on his face tied my stomach into knots, and my palms began to sweat. An evil presence seemed to be pouring into the room, dirty and defiling. As it washed over me, my body began to tremble uncontrollably from head to foot and did not stop for the next two hours. The fear was so intense that I felt I was going to vomit—and had to keep swallowing in order not to.

Alarm bells went off in my head. This doesn't happen. Something's wrong.

Oh God, get me out of here. I'm scared of this man—and this evil spirit. Please get me out of here and safely back home.

The Lord seemed to answer me, *Am I your servant, to do your will, or are you Mine?*

I'm Yours.

Then stay here. I have something for you to say to this man.

All I could think was, *I hope it's a short stay.*

The man sat down on the floor facing me, deliberately near and intimidating. With his knees almost touching me, he leaned forward and put his face closely up to mine. He was seething, but his speech was measured and restrained. "So. Are you a Muslim?"

I swallowed back another rise of nausea. "No, sir. Are you?"

Leaving niceties, he got to his point, "Yes, I am, thank God! And here's why you'd better be . . ." For the next two hours he detailed the sufferings and tortures that my family and I deserved for trying to lead Muslims away from their religion. He made threats, including sexual threats, and I turned my eyes toward Jamila. She never left my side, God bless her, but her eyes were still fastened to the floor. She was greatly ashamed to have such things done in her home, to her friend, yet she was powerless to do anything about it.

I had no idea whether this man intended to carry out his threats, whether there were in fact others like him waiting nearby, or if I was going to be taken away somewhere. My thoughts turned to my family at home. Had other angry Muslims gone there tonight in a coordinated plan against us? Was my family already experiencing the kind of harm he was describing? Would I see them again?

Later I would learn that my tormentor's name was Hamdan and that he was one of Jamila's sons, brother to the SIA agent. Known for his explosive nature, his name was used by adults in the community to frighten unruly children into obedience. "Do as we say or we'll call Hamdan al Aziiz to deal with you!"

For some reason, Hamdan gave me three opportunities to speak that night. It was just like the Bible says, "Do not worry about how or what you should speak. For it will be given to you in that hour what you should speak" (Matthew 10:19). God really did have something to say to this man, and when He said it, Hamdan was visibly and powerfully affected.

It was just like the Bible says, "Do not worry about how or what you should speak. For it will be given to you in that hour what you should speak."

My Arabic wasn't any better then than it is now, and Hamdan was using a lot of words I'd never heard. Jamila whispered audible subtitles in simpler Arabic to help. Suddenly he stopped and demanded, "What do you say to that!"

At that moment a very clear reply came into my mind. I knew it was from God because I wouldn't have thought of it on my own. "Mister Hamdan, if what you're saying is true—then I need to become a Muslim right now."

My answer seemed to defuse him slightly. "That's what I'm telling you. You need to become a Muslim right now."

"I just have one question. How can I be sure that the

Quran is true? All my life I've believed the Bible is God's Word. I've read it many times and never found anything wrong in it. Everything it prophesies comes true. The principles in it work. When I obey them I get the blessings it promises, and when I break them I get the consequences. I've actually seen answers to my prayers. All these things seem to prove the Bible is God's Word. So, if the Quran is really God's Word, then it must have even better evidence than that, right? I don't want to go to Hell or suffer the punishments you are describing. How can I know for sure that the Quran is really the Truth?"

"You want to know what evidence we have that the Quran is the Word of God? You want to know? I'll tell you. You want to know?" He was leaning back and pointing his finger at me. "You want to know why I believe the Quran is God's Word?"

Actually, I hadn't asked about his personal faith—was that the Holy Spirit directing the thoughts of this man's heart?

"I'll tell you. You want to know?" Now he was pounding his finger into the carpet as if to emphasize a point, but the point wouldn't come. Unable to think of a single piece of evidence for the Quran's validity, and perhaps feeling a bit undone by the sudden turn of events, he threw the spotlight off of himself and back onto me, shouting, "You talk in circles!"

Talking in circles? Here was a person offering to become

a Muslim if given evidence that the Quran is true. Most of my Muslim friends make up evidence. The end justifies the means. If a story gets people to embrace Islam, what difference does it make whether it's true or not? Even the newspapers print stories of supposed "evidence" to encourage the masses to remain true to Islam. There was one about a girl who refused to do *salaat* ritual prayers and turned into a dog. Witnesses saw a baby reciting the Quran as he emerged from his mother's womb. A man cut open a melon and the seeds inside spelled "Islam." But Hamdan was blank.

My body was still trembling with fear, yet in my spirit I felt hope. Did God intend to save this man's soul? This was apparently the first time Hamdan had ever questioned his own faith. This was eternal life or eternal death we were talking about. What exactly was he putting his trust in, and why? I would have been too terrified to challenge him with those kinds of questions, but God knew how to get Hamdan to ask them of himself. And He did it in a way that actually took me off the "foe" list and placed me on Hamdan's side. After all, if the Quran really were true and the Bible false, I *should* become a Muslim. It was ingenious!

I would have been too terrified to challenge him with those kinds of questions, but God knew how to get Hamdan to ask them of himself.

The second time Hamdan asked me to speak was in response to the assertion that the Bible had been corrupted over time by evil men and that Muhammad was sent to give the Quran as a replacement. A question came into my mind, posed through a story.

"Mister Hamdan, let's suppose a car accident happened in the street and forty people were witnesses to it. They all reported different bits of the story, and some of their testimonies overlapped, but when you put it all together it made one complete account. The police then compiled it into one record and put it on file at the police department. Then, twenty years later, a man came to the police with another file and said, 'That file you have with all those witnesses' reports is incorrect. I know what really happened, I have the real truth.' Do you think the police would believe him and exchange the files?"

Arabs often use stories to express themselves, and Hamdan had listened with interest. "Of course not," he replied. "What does that have to do with anything?"

"Well, I was just wondering why my Muslim friends keep saying the Bible is corrupted. The Bible was written by forty different men over a period of 1,500 years. Some wrote about one thing and some another, while others overlapped, but when you read it all together it is one complete Truth. All of these witnesses over all these centuries have agreed. Then one man, the prophet Muhammad, comes along and the whole Arab World forsakes the old record to follow the Quran. Why?"

The evening was going much differently than either of us could ever have anticipated. God really had had something to say to this man, and with loving-kindness He'd gently opened Hamdan's ears to hear it.

In the end, Hamdan stood up to leave. He had not laid a finger on me. "The last word is this . . ." he began. By prefacing his closing remarks this way, he conveyed that he expected no further conversation. "The last word is that you are going directly to Hell, and everyone who follows you in this Way is going directly to Hell. And that will be on your head. Forever." He paused, looking down at me. "Last word."

Although I knew what "last word" meant, and I certainly didn't want to do anything to revive his lessened anger, one *last* last word came into my mind. I immediately knew it was from the Lord and why I had to say it.

"Thank you."

Hamdan froze at first. Then, he looked at me incredulously. Almost in a whisper he hissed, *"What?!"* The dissipated rage now gave way to disbelief.

"Well, you've just spent two hours of your time trying to convince me to become a Muslim because you really believe that if I don't I'll go to Hell. So I can only think that you're trying to save my soul. And for that, I thank you." I meant it too. Slowly Hamdan backed away toward the door, shaking his head and fanning his two hands up and down in the air as if pushing himself away from me. When he left, the evil spirit went with him.

As soon as he was gone, I was ready to bolt. However, my body had turned to butter. Jamila had to help me up but still couldn't look me in the eye. She kept asking my forgiveness and I kept telling her it wasn't her fault; I knew she and the others had had to obey the men. Nevertheless, deep inside I did feel betrayed, and it had hurt. It would be weeks before I had the emotional strength to visit those women again. Little did I realize how glad I'd be that I went back. It was the return visit that would give the events of this night a sudden and dramatic twist none of us were expecting.

It was the return visit that would give the events of this night a sudden and dramatic twist none of us were expecting.

Rushing into our house, I was relieved and grateful to find my family peacefully asleep in their beds. Immediately I spoiled that for Mike, waking him up to sob all over him as the whole story gushed out. We prayed together for some time, and he was very comforting. But after having been in the presence of that filthy spirit for so long, I actually had to take a shower and then spend a few hours reading the Bible just to feel "clean" and safe enough to go to sleep.

Several weeks later there I was, sitting on the floor in Mozi's *majlis* surrounded by all the women of the family (except Jamila, who happened to be visiting a neighbor when I'd arrived). As we were exchanging idle chitchat about recipes and nail polish, the door opened and in walked Hamdan. It quickly became obvious that he had not known the ladies had a guest. He was just passing through the *majlis* to the other end of the house. How different he looked! Here in the broad daylight and surrounded by people, he wasn't angry and that evil presence wasn't with him. For the first time I realized he was actually about a head shorter than me. He almost looked boyish. Suddenly God filled my heart with compassion for him, and I felt that all his violent exterior was protection for the frightened soul within. I almost wanted to hug him and tell him how much Jesus loved him.

I didn't.

Seeming to waffle for a moment over what to do, he stepped into the midst of his female kin and sat down. "So, Reema, have you become a Muslim yet?"

Wanting to be friends, I light-heartedly replied, "No, Mister Hamdan . . . have you become a Christian yet?"

He smiled a genuine smile. Then he asked a question

WHICH NONE CAN SHUT

related to the Bible. It seemed the best way to answer him was to share the story of how I'd become a *mu'mina*, a believer, myself. When I finished, Mozi patted my leg and very seriously asked, "Is that story true?"

"Yes, it is. And God will do the same for you if you will believe in His Son." How many times had I told that story, yet this time it seemed to touch her.

Hamdan stood up and resumed his commanding demeanor. "Reema!"

"Yes, Mister Hamdan."

"Do you have this Bible of yours in Arabic?"

"Yes, sir."

"Bring it to me. If I'm not here, leave it and I'll come get it. I want to see this 'Bible' of yours." He said it with disdain, but he'd asked!

The next day I wrapped an Arabic Bible in cloth and brought it over. Jamila, who hadn't heard the request, was the only one there to receive it, and this fact would become significant later. Being illiterate herself, she couldn't tell it was a Bible. I gave her the book, simply saying that Hamdan had asked for it. Our family had gotten things for them before, so she had no reason to wonder about it.

A few weeks later Jamila and I were making small talk as we sat together on a hospital room floor, spending time with her sick niece, when she mentioned the book.

"Oh, you know that book that you brought for Hamdan? Well, he likes it."

I was startled. *He likes it? Does she know what she's telling me? It's a Bible, for goodness sake!*

Jamila went on, almost complaining about her son's interest in it, "Actually, he likes it a lot. You know, when he comes home from work, all he does anymore is read, read, read that book!"

Since then, Mike and I have had other positive encounters with Hamdan. He has accepted Bibles, study material, Christian media, and literature from us secretly and is such a changed person that we believe him to be a secret believer. With a big smile he shakes Mike's hand and introduces him to other Muslims as his friend. When we visit the family home, Hamdan serves us food from the generously laden *fou'alla* tray himself, honoring us. One day we hope to hear the whole story from Hamdan's perspective and to learn just how he became a *mu'min* himself.

✦ ✦ ✦

Even before our arrival in Arabia, we were warned about surveillance. It was better not to draw attention to ourselves since any Christian activity

Even before our arrival in Arabia, we were warned not to draw attention to ourselves since any Christian activity might be monitored.

might be monitored. Our phones might be tapped, mail read, and trash picked through. In fact, some of our mail has arrived with a government stamp on it, letting us know that it has been opened and read. We have had trash disappear from the bin. Our phones certainly seem to be tapped, what with all the clicking and confused sounds in the background disturbing our conversations. Nevertheless, not all of our fears have been realized, or warranted.

Once while we were living in an apartment building, the need arose to dispose of some "sensitive material." Since we couldn't risk letting anything be found in our trash that might incriminate us as Christian missionaries, we decided to burn it. Have you ever started a fire in an apartment? Talk about not drawing attention to ourselves! We used an empty coffee can in the kitchen sink so we'd have water if things got out of hand. As soon as the papers caught fire we realized our mistake. Smoke began billowing out our kitchen window. People in the street began to look up. It was an inordinate amount of smoke for so little paper. The people began pointing, with expressions of concern on their faces. What if one of them called the fire department and we had to explain why we were burning papers in a coffee can?

Another somewhat humorous experience happened to Mike while he was in language training. Tired of studying at his desk, he decided to take his language cards outside and go for a walk.

The cards all had simple sentences from his lesson on them, in Arabic, and he practiced reading them out loud. First, "Where is the bag?" Then, "Is the bag here?" Then, "The bag is there." As he went along, he came to a low brick wall, stopped, and rested his elbows on it as he reviewed a few more sentences.

Out of nowhere three Arab men approached him, probably plainclothes police. Though they didn't speak English, they communicated that they wanted to know what he was doing. Mike tried to explain that he was just practicing his Arabic, but he didn't have enough of the language yet to make himself clear. Seeing their growing impatience and not knowing what else to do, he decided to just show them. In his best Arabic, Mike read the first card out loud, "Where is the bag?" The three men started looking around with puzzled expressions, apparently looking for the bag. Attempting to clarify his demonstration, he read the second card. "Is the bag here?" The men started talking to each other, perplexed. Again Mike read, "The bag is there." All three men came and leaned over the wall, looking for the bag!

Suddenly, a walkie-talkie that had been concealed in one of the men's pockets came on. He pulled it out and had a hurried conversation with someone. Then, with a disdainful look at Mike and some hand gestures, they ran off. Mike actually came home encouraged by this encounter—at least they had understood his Arabic.

✢

Ask, and it will be given to you.

MATTHEW 7:7

CHAPTER 3

The Power of Questions

"Excuse me." The princess lifted a graceful hand and pointed across the ornately decorated palace *majlis* at me. Seated on a lovely couch, she was flanked on either side by other royal ladies.

A number of visitors had come to see her that day, all seated in a semicircle of beautiful furniture facing Her Highness and being attended to by a squad of servants. One heavily laden tray after another of delicious morsels and artistically presented beverages had been brought around the room and offered to each guest by turn. Who could outdo an Arab royal family when it comes to hospitality? With all of the visitors she was making conversation with, and all of the serving going on, I had hoped the princess wouldn't notice that I hadn't had anything. After all, it's an offense to any Arab if you refuse his hospitality; how much more so to refuse the generosity of a royal?

"Excuse me." Several of the visitors became quiet and turned to see whom their royal host was addressing. "Why aren't you drinking my coffee?"

I certainly didn't want to appear to be rejecting the friendship of the princess, but I had no choice. God had told me to fast that day. He was the one who'd gotten me into this predicament and He was the one who would have to get me out.

Of course, the fact that I was a guest at a palace in the first place was God's doing. I'm just a girl from Nowheresville, USA. Three of us Christian women were being permitted to call on her that day, but I can't explain why for reasons of security.

God was the one who'd gotten me into this predicament and He was the one who would have to get me out.

At home earlier that morning, I'd been making a mental list of preparations for the occasion. *Okay, I have to do my hair, iron my clothes, have breakfast . . .* It seemed as if God interrupted my thoughts and said, *Fast today.*

I can't fast today, I reasoned with Him in my mind. *I'm going to see a princess. That would be an insult to the royal family.* (As if God doesn't understand Arab culture?) Still,

it just didn't make sense to fast at a time like this. *Fast today—*
the thought wouldn't go away.

When I met to pray with the two other Christian women
who were going on the visit, I told them my dilemma. After
all, this would reflect on them too. After some discussion and
prayer, both Sheila and Jane encouraged me to go ahead and
do what I felt God was telling me to do.

So there we were, the three of us seated together on one
large sofa with a royal question hanging in the air. No words
of wisdom from the Lord came into my mind, so I decided
to just plain tell her and let the responsibility fall on God's
shoulders for what He was having me do. "Please forgive me,
Princess, but I am fasting today."

She looked surprised. "Christians fast? I didn't know that.
How do you fast? You mean you just won't eat meat today,
but you'll have rice."

"Well, no, I won't eat anything."

"You'll drink juice?"

"No, I won't eat or drink anything but water today."
Muslims sometimes feel their method of fasting is superior
because they eat or drink nothing whatsoever from sunup
until sundown. As soon as I said that I would drink water,
I could see the slight smirks and nods of others in the room,
who were politely observing the dialogue.

Quickly I continued, "Actually, there are many ways

Christians fast. Many Arab believers fast in just the same way you do. This morning God told me to fast today, so I committed to eat nothing and drink only water from this morning until tomorrow morning. A full twenty-four-hour day."

The princess looked at me squarely. "You mean that tonight you will go to bed hungry?" The atmosphere in the room seemed to change.

"Yes." This was a significant fact simply because sundown is supposed to be when a fast ends and feasting starts.

Her interest was sparked, and suddenly other questions she'd had about Christian beliefs and practice came to her

Her interest was sparked, and suddenly other questions she'd had about Christian beliefs and practice came to her mind, like "How can Jesus be God?"

mind, like "How can Jesus be God?" Sheila and Jane began to respond to her questions, too, and soon a serious spiritual conversation had begun among the four of us. At the same time, a *majlis* full of visitors and a bevy of servants were also hearing the Truth. One subject led to another, and everyone seemed to be listening. No doubt other Muslims in the room had had the same questions. Jane, being more adept in the language, did a great job of explaining things. Sheila also shared well, and her special relationship with the princess gave the three of us credibility.

This was an amazing opportunity. After all, if an Arab Muslim princess was spiritually seeking, whom would she talk to? Where could she go? Royal women are guarded, watched, and accompanied. Personal drivers and bodyguards are assigned to protect and escort these *hareem*, or "forbidden ones." The royal men have access to whatever intelligence and security measures money can buy. Mobile phone and computer signals are easily intercepted, and household servants can eavesdrop on private conversations. So how could such a public Muslim figure possibly express interest in the tenets of Christianity in front of all these witnesses? Wouldn't the princess get into trouble talking to us like this?

Again, God is ingenious. He'd given the princess a perfect cover to ask any question she'd ever had about Christianity from a panel of three Christians right there in her own home, and He had done it in such a way that would keep us all from any negative repercussions. Because fasting is considered a noble religious act toward God, it is perhaps the only unoffensive reason for not eating or drinking with one's host. When she let me explain my fast in front of everyone, she was graciously and publicly letting me off the hook. This actually reflected well on her benevolence, demonstrating the basis for her royal forgiveness toward the clumsy American, whose refusal of hospitality in this culture would normally have had serious negative implications. At the same time, the incident provided her with a perfect excuse to hear about her visitors' Christian beliefs and practice. She was just being diplomatic. Who could find fault with that? Ingenious.

In our family's experience, the door of opportunity seems to be shaped like a question mark. Sometimes the question

In our family's experience, the door of opportunity seems to be shaped like a question mark.

to ask is dropped into our laps, as in the case of the Islamic holiday *Eid al Adha*. It's not only an important occasion for visiting everyone you know, but it comes with a built-in spiritual conversation starter. We found this out at Habiiba's house when I went to visit the women for the *Eid*. As the oldest daughter in her father's home, she was responsible for the huge amount of cooking and other household preparations that needed to be made, so her sister Noora sat with me in the *majlis*.

"What is *Eid al Adha*?" I inquired with genuine interest. (Starting a spiritual conversation probably doesn't get any easier than that.) Noora, a very down-to-earth person and mature beyond her teenage years, was happy as always to tell me more about Islam. Normally, she deferred to her older sister in conversation out of respect, but today that would not be necessary. She fairly lit up at the opportunity to answer my question herself.

"In this holiday we remember the story of our Master Abraham, peace be upon him. He was told in a dream that he was to sacrifice Ishmael, his oldest son, and when he woke up he did so."

She continued on emphasizing the point that it was Ishmael, not Isaac, as though she expected me to take issue with that. But I was intrigued by the fact that this story was in the Quran. "You mean Abraham actually sacrificed him?"

Noora quickly changed gears, "No, no! He had the boy on the altar and was about to kill him as a sacrifice, but God stopped him."

Amazing! I had to know more. "Is that it? He just told him to stop? What happened?" Somehow my enthusiasm seemed to diminish Noora's. "Well, God stopped him and then sent down a ram out of Heaven to be a replacement sacrifice."

A ram out of Heaven!

This was astounding. God had seen to it that a ray of Gospel light had been recorded in the Quran! "And why do you celebrate this? What does the story mean to Muslims?"

Now it was Noora's turn to ask a

This was astounding. God had seen to it that a ray of Gospel light had been recorded in the Quran!

question, "What do you mean, 'What does it mean'? It's just something we do to remember the story. It doesn't mean anything." Looking at me quizzically she continued, "What are you getting at?"

"Well, it just seems like such a big celebration would have to have a reason behind it, some meaning to it. This story is in the Bible as well, and it is considered very important because it has such a powerful and beautiful meaning. All the stories in the Bible have a deep, connected meaning."

We looked at each other for a moment. Now another question was hanging in the air, just begging to be asked. Finally, she asked it. "What's the meaning?"

I can't express the joy it was to tell her.

"Remember in Eden, how Adam and Eve ate the forbidden fruit? God said that if they ate it they would die. Death of the body and death of the soul eternally. God loved them and wanted them to live in Heaven with Him forever, but He's holy and never breaks His Word. He'd said that the penalty for sin was death, and there was no changing it. Instead, He made it possible for someone else to take the death penalty for them. He promised to send a Substitute down from Heaven one day, to die in place of sinful people. That way He could forgive them without breaking His Word. This story is a symbol, a picture of that promise.

"God said that Abraham's son had to die, just like He

says sinners have to die. God stopped the son's death and sent a ram from Heaven to take his place, just as He stops our death by sending a Substitute from Heaven to take our place. Dear Noora, don't you see? That's why Jesus is called the Lamb . . . the 'Lamb of God who takes away the sin of the world.' He is the ram sent down from Heaven to die for us! Jesus sacrificed Himself to fulfill our death sentence. All who believe and confess Him are forgiven, and allowed into Heaven with God forever!"

I could hardly contain myself. Just telling the Gospel through the vivid imagery of that story was a thrill in itself. But there was more to rejoice about. There were tears emerging from Noora's beautiful, dark eyes and lodging in her lashes. She understood. I think it was the first time she had really understood.

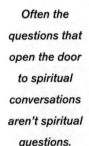

Often the questions that open the door to spiritual conversations aren't spiritual questions.

✦ ✦ ✦

Often the questions that open the door to spiritual conversations aren't spiritual questions. My relationship with Salama began over a discussion about current events. She'd sat down beside me in a waiting area to try out her English. We introduced ourselves and as usual the first question was "Where are you from?"

"You are from America? Then you should see the newspaper today. I think there will be nothing left of your country soon. Floods, fires, earthquakes, hurricanes . . . Also Africa still is having famine after all these years. And now the East has tsunami! The whole world is coming apart."

"You're right," I agreed. "I guess the only good thing about it is that it's a sign Jesus is coming back soon. The Bible says there will be a dramatic increase in natural disasters all over the world right before His return. Doesn't the Quran say something like that too?"

"Yes, it does. We also believe that Jesus is coming back at the end of times. But you believe He died on the cross and we believe He did not die . . ." Just then, the lady I was with finished her business and got up to leave. As I excused myself, Salama grabbed her pen, "Wait, give me your mobile number. You must come to my house so we can talk more about this." During our last conversation, she asked if she could introduce me to a friend of hers who might like to join our spiritual discussions.

To us, it doesn't really matter if the person we are sharing with is a genuine seeker or an openly hostile fundamentalist, because the Word of God itself is living and powerful. It has an effect on people whether they believe in it or not! And though we might not get a chance to present the whole "plan of salvation" per se, if we share any kind of Truth from God's

Word, we've done something. Knowing we are only one link in a chain of events that our completely sovereign God is in total control of takes all the pressure off! Hallelujah! Even more exciting is how He confirms the Truth He's allowed us to share. One great example of this is the story of Sadiiq, our realtor.

Knowing we are only one link in a chain of events that our completely sovereign God is in total control of takes all the pressure off! Hallelujah!

Mike hired Sadiiq to help us locate a new home in the area, and they had already spent a good amount of time together looking at prospective rentals. Our family was praying for an opportunity to share with him, and Mike had tried to broach the subject of spiritual things a number of different ways, but Sadiiq seemed disinterested. Little did we imagine how God was about to get his attention.

On a trip to negotiate with one of the landlords, Sadiiq was in the front passenger seat giving directions to Mike as he was driving. I was sitting in the back, having a conversation about the meanings of various Arabic names with him in between turns. "Mr. Sadiiq, our Arab friends tell us that there are one hundred names for God. Ninety-nine of them are in the Quran, and the hundredth is known only to the camel. They say that's why camels are so arrogant."

He laughed out loud at that one, "No, it's not true. They

only tell that to tourists! There is no one hundredth name of God."

We chuckled too. "Well, it may not be true about the camel, but there really is a hundredth name of God. Technically it's His first name, since the ninety-nine are actually titles. It's in our Book, the Bible."

Of course it was only natural that he would ask the next question. "Really? I've never heard this before. What is it?"

In Arabic, I quoted the name of God revealed to Moses in Exodus 3:14, "I AM WHO I AM."

Suddenly, Sadiiq's expression changed. He cocked his ear toward me to hear better. "What did you say?" I repeated the name. His jaw dropped and his eyes widened. Mike and I were both wondering what was going on. Clearly something was happening here. He was visibly affected. Again he asked, "What did you say?" Five times he made me repeat it. I pronounced it slower, thinking that maybe my Arabic wasn't clear and I was saying something wrong. By the fifth time Sadiiq was completely turned around in his seat, facing me. Slowly he raised his hand, pointed his finger in my face, and blurted out, "I think this is the truth!"

Mike and I both had the same exact thought, *You do? Why?!* After all, we hadn't really told him anything yet. That was just the name!

Sadiiq continued, "Sometimes I know something is true in

my heart before I understand why with my head. And that name . . . when you say that name . . . I feel something . . . coming on my body . . . like a force!"

Since that day, Sadiiq has been a regular visitor at our house. He has done a Bible survey study with Mike from Genesis to Jesus, is reading the Bible for himself, and calls up with questions. When he comes over at eight or nine in the evening he usually doesn't leave until one or two in the morning. Mike and I joke that by the time Sadiiq converts, he'll be a qualified Bible teacher!

Another great example of God confirming His Word to Muslim hearts is Sana. Our paths crossed through a string of events, which were set into motion late one night when I asked God a question.

We'd just had a prayer meeting in our home that lasted until midnight, and now it was cleanup time. Besides all the usual tidying up, there was a pile of dishes to do. Mike took the kids upstairs to put them to bed and never came down. He had meant to come back down to help but accidentally fell asleep beside one of the kids. Even though we'd been praying for hours, I was somehow still unspiritual enough to be irked. Standing at the sink, I poured out my complaint. As I was going on and on (and on), the Lord suddenly seemed to interrupt me, *Maybe I wanted you down here doing dishes all alone at one o'clock in the morning.*

WHICH NONE CAN SHUT

Of all the ways to lay blame for my suffering, that one hadn't crossed my mind. Dropping several notches on my irk-o-meter, I rather sheepishly inquired, *Uh, why would You want that?* God didn't answer. Immediately I knew that unless some speedy repentance took place here, I wasn't going to find out. I concluded my confession with a request, *Lord, please forgive my complaining thoughts and replace them with Your thoughts. Direct my mind onto the things You want me to be thinking about right now instead.* Ideas started coming into my mind so fast that I had to take off my rubber gloves and go into the office to write them down.

I was to start a Christian home gathering open to Muslim women. It would be a safe place where they could come and see what Christians do. (Most ladies would never dream of entering a public church building—not only is it "Christian" but there are men there as well.) It would be during normal visiting hours so that anyone might attend without being made suspect. I should provide a stack of Arabic Bibles and sheets of Arabic songs to sing. These items could be kept at our house so that the women wouldn't have any "paraphernalia" to worry about. God seemed to be giving me a commission: ". . . and when they come into your home, teach them how to worship Me."

It was to this gathering that Sana came, invited by an Arab Christian friend named Alia at work. She came, not because

56

of any interest in Christianity, but because she was dying. A young and beautiful career woman in her thirties, Sana had so much life in her. She had a bright future, a wonderful husband who truly loved her, and children they both adored. She also had a malignant tumor growing inside her brain. Weekly tests were made to monitor its growth, but there was no way to actually stop it. The doctors had frankly said that it would progress to blindness, paralysis, and finally death. Although we were all aware of Sana's circumstances, none of us mentioned it to her when she came. It seemed better to just extend our loving friendship and let her bring it up when she felt comfortable.

Partway through the meeting, Sana spoke up. "My friend Alia is always telling us at work about this group. She says you pray for each other and God answers your prayers. She says you also pray for us." Briefly she smiled a thank-you to the group of women around her. "I came tonight because . . ." Her voice began to falter. Looking down at her lap, she raised a hand to her face as if ashamed to let us see the emotions that were now rushing to the surface. The other hand began to search frantically in her

Looking down at her lap, she raised a hand to her face as if ashamed to let us see the emotions that were now rushing to the surface.

purse for a tissue, then emerged clutching it. "Can you pray for me? The doctors say there is nothing they can do. . . ."

When Sana burst into tears, so did the rest of us. We got up off our seats and surrounded her in prayer, a hand holding hers, an arm around her shoulder.

"Dear Father God, we believe that You brought Sana here tonight because You love her and want to heal her body and her spirit. You know all about what she and her family are going through, and You care. Heavenly Father, we ask You to heal Sana completely of every trace of disease in her body, in the name of the Lord Jesus Christ. Let Your healing of Sana demonstrate to her that You are real and that You want her to know You personally. Show her that the things she has read and heard here tonight from Your Word are true, and give her faith to believe and be saved."

In the sovereignty of God, the next day happened to be Sana's weekly checkup. Her doctor read the results of the tests and frowned. Ridiculous. The lab people must be incompetent. "Run them again," he told the nurse. The tests were repeated and came out the same. Further tests were ordered, until the doctor was finally convinced that the killer tumor really was nowhere to be found. "I don't know what's happened here, but you don't have a tumor anymore. You're healed. Tell my secretary to cancel your future appointments." Unwittingly, the Muslim doctor had just provided thorough medical documentation that the Christians' prayer had been answered!

That day, Alia received a jubilant phone call from the ecstatic couple. As Sana shared the whole story in detail, Alia could hear her husband in the background shouting, "Tell them we're with them! Tell them we're with them!" Immediately they expressed an interest to meet with Alia and her husband privately to learn more about this Way.

How great is our God?

✛

Preach the word! Be ready
in season and out of season.
Convince, rebuke, exhort, with all
longsuffering and teaching.

2 TIMOTHY 4:2

CHAPTER 4

When You Least Expect It

Not one invitation but two! Two invitations to dinner at the palatial home of Mr. VIP, each given to us by a different local friend. How did Mike and I ever rate such an honor? Actually, we didn't. All you had to do to be invited to this particular kind of dinner party was to be a non-Muslim. Just one of many good works that Mr. VIP's wealth sponsored, the dinner was a way of spreading Islam and hopefully securing Mr. VIP additional merit in the eyes of Allah. It was a thinly disguised evangelistic event.

Basically, an open invitation was made to the local Muslim population. They were welcome to attend a special dinner at Mr. VIP's mansion, provided they bring a non-Muslim with them as a potential convert. Most citizens of Little Town could never hope to see such a grandiose residence from the inside, let alone enjoy a meal with the master of the house, and foreigners were even less likely candidates. The invitation was meant to be alluring, and it worked. Two of our local friends had invited us.

Enticing as it was, there was a downside. Muslim outreaches could be very controlled. They didn't seem to afford the opportunity to share Christ the way ordinary visits did. Calling on a couple of humble neighborhood homes seemed a much better investment of our time, as far as sharing the Gospel was concerned. When something suddenly came up that prevented Mike from going, I was more than happy to change plans too.

These outreaches by Muslims could be very controlled. They didn't seem to afford the opportunity to share Christ the way ordinary visits did.

"No, I still think you should go." Mike used the soft, husbandly tone of voice that was reserved for just such occasions. That is, an occasion where he was about to counsel me to do something I really didn't want to do.

"But why? These public outreach schemes are all the same. We've heard it all before. At least if I go on a private visit, I can get a chance to share with somebody."

"I don't know why, but I really feel that you should go to this one." God had often led me through just such "feelings" of his; it was not something to be taken lightly. Clasping my hand, Mike continued, "Let me pray for you . . ." He ended his prayer with a special request, "Lord, I ask You to please give Reema the blessing of being able to share with someone tonight—maybe even with the whole group. In Jesus' name, Amen."

The Bible says that if two believers agree about anything on earth it will be done for them, but I have to admit I wasn't "agreeing" with Mike's prayer at that particular moment. I was actually thinking, *Yeah, right. As if God would give me the chance to share the Gospel at a Muslim evangelistic event.*

To my amazement, that is exactly what He did.

That evening, a bustling crowd of zealous young ladies escorted female visitors into the luxurious women's *majlis* to await the entrance of Mrs. VIP. Somehow, the forty or more Muslim ladies present had only managed to bring two unbelievers. We recognized each other—Diane and I were fellow missionaries! With a gesture, she let me know she'd be praying for me, and I did the same. Then an escalation in the crowd's fervor announced the entrance of Mrs. VIP.

She was lovely, a picture of gracious femininity. Each guest was brought before her for a personal welcome and then escorted to a comfortable seat. Lastly, she seated herself, and coffee was served. Immediately, her cell phone rang. Excusing herself to take the call, Mrs. VIP left and never came back. In walked Fatima the Fundamentalist, our master of ceremonies and featured speaker for the evening.

Fatima was a harsh-looking older woman who appeared to relish her job. Her reddened face contorted with pleasure as she lambasted Christian doctrine, slandered the Bible, and blasphemed the Lord Jesus Christ. The predinner program was to last two hours and was not exactly what you would call "friendship evangelism."

Fatima's reddened face contorted with pleasure as she lambasted Christian doctrine, slandered the Bible, and blasphemed the Lord Jesus Christ.

The agenda alternated between Fatima's caustic monologues and personal testimonies by converts to Islam. The converts and even the audience seemed intimidated by their leader's vehemence. The veins in her temples grew larger, and droplets of saliva shot out as she seethed, "You Western women think you are so intelligent because you are well-educated. The fact is that you have been duped into worshiping a man as a god and believing a book that our Islamic scholars say has at least fifty errors on every page! If you had half a brain in your head and would use it for just five minutes, you would become Muslim!"

Now, in reality, the same arguments had been raised many times by our friends, yet in a very different spirit. When they said we believed foolish lies, we knew it was because they actually cared about us and didn't want us to go to Hell. Their genuine concern had drawn our hearts closer to them. Fatima was a different story altogether. How dare this woman? She was even twisting and perverting the Scriptures to back up her erroneous arguments! As I watched her yelling and shaking her finger in Diane's face, my blood began to boil. Feeling the anger rise, I cried out to God in my heart.

Lord, I'm afraid that if she shakes that bony finger in my face I'm going to let her have it! Please don't let me blow years of walking with You in front of these people by losing it all over Fatima right now. Help me!

Immediately a verse came to mind, "The wrath of man does not produce the righteousness of God" (James 1:20).

Okay. Right. Wrath isn't going to help anything. But what do I do?

Another verse came: "A servant of the Lord must not quarrel but be gentle to all, able to teach" (2 Timothy 2:24).

Able to teach! Suddenly it dawned on me. Mike's prayer! All at once I understood why I was there, why I'd had to come. Every shred of anger disappeared and was replaced with joyful anticipation. For the rest of the

All at once I understood why I was there, why I'd had to come. Every shred of anger disappeared and was replaced with joyful anticipation.

evening my prayer was this, *Oh God, don't let me leave this place without giving them the chance to hear the Gospel. There is an answer to every single thing that Fatima has said. Let these people hear Your Truth tonight as it really is, untwisted, unperverted, and uninterrupted. And stop the mouths of the "gainsayers"!*

Two hours later, all the testimonies had been shared and Fatima was in her closing argument. Her face was nearly purple from the effort she was exerting to drive her point home. Stepping in front of me, she shook her finger in my face for emphasis.

"It is obvious that you Christians are not the people of God because you're all so different. We Muslims all dress the same and pray the same. We're unified. You're inconsistent! For one thing, some of you drink and some of you don't drink. What does the Bible actually say about alcohol?"

So confident that this was a God-given opportunity, I was able to reply cheerily. "That's a good question, but before I answer it I'd just like to say thank you to everyone for inviting us here tonight. I have learned so much about what Muslims think and what you think we think. I have to say that there does seem to be a basic misconception as to what a Christian actually is and how you become one. Would you mind if I just sort of cleared that up first?"

There was silence. Some of the women looked at each

other. Finally, somebody said, "Sure, go ahead." So I did, trying to cover as many other bases as possible in the process:

- The Bible is not an Old Jewish Testament and a New Christian Gospel; it is one book with a single message.
- The creation and fall of man in Genesis established both our need for a Redeemer and God's promise to send one.
- The whole Old Testament, either directly or indirectly, points us to this One who is coming to reconcile us to God and restore the relationship with Him that was lost.
- The New Testament tells us the good news that this Redeemer came, fulfilling all of the prophesies, just as God promised.
- A Christian is someone who believes what God did and has submitted to His way of reconciliation through that Redeemer, Jesus the Messiah.

A lady raised her hand, "Where in the Bible does it say that Jesus is God?"

Nothing like cutting right to the chase! One of the teenagers handed me a Bible, which had just been used to demonstrate "errors" in the text. Opening to the first verse, I read aloud to the now attentive group, "In the beginning God created . . ."

Reading on, I emphasized the repetitive theme: God *said*, and it was . . . God *said*, and it was. Turning to John 1, the *Word* of God made everything, the Word of God *is God*, the Word of God *became flesh* and walked among us: Jesus.

Hands shot up all around the room and women slid to the edge of their seats, leaning forward. God was turning this Muslim evangelistic event into a forum for proclaiming the Gospel! The question-and-answer period lasted for forty minutes, and two things became crystal clear: the women had been thinking about these things for a long time, and Fatima's arguments hadn't satisfied them.

At this point, the ardent leader tried to stand up, finger outstretched, mouth open, but no words were coming out. It appeared that God really was stopping her mouth! He also had a helper, in the form of a woman seated beside Fatima who kept swatting at her and saying, "Shhh! Sit down! We want to hear the Christian!"

"Shhh! Sit down! We want to hear the Christian!"

Sensing the embarrassment that the sudden turn of events had caused, and not wanting any hard feelings, it seemed wise to preserve the bond of peace by helping Fatima and the sponsors of the event to save face. "I'm sorry to have taken so much of your time tonight," I offered meekly. "This is your evening, and we're supposed to be talking about Islam."

One woman quickly dismissed my apology. "Oh no, not at all, this has been wonderful! We've been coming to events like these for years and this is the first time that we've heard Christian beliefs explained by an actual Christian."

Just as I was offering to have a Bible study at my home for anyone interested in reading more for themselves, dinner was announced. Ladies jumped up, but instead of getting in line for the buffet, they gathered tightly around me. Several were asking questions all at once. I was stunned. How amazing that the supporters of the Islamic outreach dinner would be so hungry for the Living Bread!

Stories like this are not unique to our family by any means. At a recent peer conference of Christian workers in the Arab Muslim World, people from every country represented had amazing stories like these. The volume and frequency has increased every year for the past decade, marking what seems to be a growing trend in ministry to Muslims. One new worker who came to our area was frustrated by the amount of time it would take her to learn to speak the language. She prayed for her neighbors but felt sure it would be ages before she could hope to share meaningfully with them. One day there was a knock at her door. When she opened it, there were five women standing at the threshold, waiting to ask her a question.

"Are you a Christian?"

"Yes . . ." The worker marveled that her very first conversation with Arab Muslim neighbors should start like this.

"Do you have a Bible?"

"Yes, I do."

"Well, we've been talking and have decided that we want to read the Bible together, for ourselves. If you let us use your Bible, then you can come too."

So now we have the Muslims inviting the missionary to their Bible study. Is God at work in the Arab World?

We are all on a big learning curve as we are coming to expect the unexpected. When Mike needed extra help learning Arabic, he was blessed to find an Arab gentleman who spoke English rather fluently. Mr. Rashid was a thoughtful and scholarly man, very well-educated, and familiar with other cultures. The two agreed on an hourly rate for tutoring, but soon found that more and more of their language study time was actually being spent on religious discussions. Mr. Rashid rather enjoyed the stimulating spiritual conversation over the dull, repetitive lesson practice, and of course was paid for his time regardless of how it was used. For Mike, it was a double blessing. He got to

We are all on a big learning curve as we are coming to expect the unexpected.

share the Gospel while getting a break from struggling with Arabic. What a deal!

It was, in any case, money very well spent. After all, the reason Mike was learning the language in the first place was to be able to share the Good News with Arab Muslims. Mr. Rashid's openness to discussion permitted Mike to skip right to the point. It became the highlight of his week, and a friendship developed.

Being analytical thinkers, each man was a challenge to the other. Their deepening discussions led to increasingly difficult questions, which in turn drove both men to their books. Mike, always an ardent Bible student, was digging through the Word more intently than ever in order to share its rich, inerrant Truth with his Muslim peer. He even taught Mr. Rashid the principles of exegesis to give them a solid, agreed-upon methodology for their study!

Their meetings went on for months. This ongoing discussion not only benefited both of them but resulted in the development of an evangelistic/discipleship tool for Christian workers to use in Muslim ministry. Mr. Rashid's arguments, challenges, questions, and other input had inspired and indispensably aided Mike's authoring of the material. Designed for use as a Bible study for Muslim seekers or a discipleship course for converts, it's also being used in churches and small groups for equipping believers to share

WHICH NONE CAN SHUT

their faith with Muslims. Although Mike never quite "got" Arabic the way he would have liked to, the value of those many months in "language study" with his tutor apparently had a far greater purpose in God's plan!

✣ ✣ ✣

Umm Abayd was a perfect stranger. I met her during a visit to a friend's house. She asked for my number and began to call and drop by our home, usually around mealtimes. After a while I got the feeling she had a whole circuit of people that she visited in order to avoid buying groceries. When I became ill from another pregnancy, I stopped having her come by. The next time I saw her was a year later. After about an hour of catching up on news, her expression turned more serious.

"I liked the film," she stated simply.

"What film?" I thought maybe she'd been to the movies recently.

"The film you gave me." I didn't recall ever giving her a film. Noticing my stupor, she leaned closer, "You know, the one about Jesus."

Apparently I'd given her the *JESUS* film, a dramatization of the Gospel of Luke. "What did you like about it?" I asked.

"Everything." She made a thumbs-up gesture and rolled back in her seat with an expression that seemed to say, "Wow!"

"Did you know this story is from the Bible?"

"Yes, the *Injil*."

"The *Injil*, the Gospel, is a part of the Bible. Do you have a whole Bible?"

"No, I don't have anything."

"Can I bring you one, next time I see you?"

"Yes, bring it."

"I also have some other things . . ."

"Bring me everything. I want more of this. I want to know everything."

+++

Another example of the unexpected is Amira, a gentle widow whose husband was rumored to have become a Christian years ago. He and his two sons had all died untimely deaths. Now elderly, Amira seemed to enjoy having visitors come to sit with her, and Sheila, Jane, and I were no exception. Although she was friendly and honored us with the same hospitality as her Muslim guests, she did make a distinction. During greetings she would cover her hand with the long end of her head scarf to keep from actually touching our hands. Sometimes, she even washed afterwards. Despite that, she kept inviting us back.

On one particular visit, there was a conversation about coffee, and I told her that the next time we came I'd bring her a pot of American brew. She seemed to find that amusing and agreed it might be fun to have a new experience. I had the feeling that receiving anything from her guests might be a new experience. Amira was viewed as well-off, and many people "visit" the wealthy looking for gifts. When American coffee and donuts were presented to her on our next visit, she was actually surprised and very well-pleased. Drinking several little cupfuls, she reminisced that her husband had liked his coffee just this way, strong and without the spices. On the next visit we grew bolder.

Although we very much wanted to offer her a Bible, it had come to light that Amira had never learned to read.

Amira could hear the Gospel in a way she was most familiar with . . . that tried-and-true Arabian venue, storytelling.

She'd grown up in a world where boys went to school only to learn to recite the Quran and girls didn't go at all. On our very next visit, we brought a gift-wrapped twelve-volume set of the dramatized Bible on tape. She could hear the Gospel in a way she was most familiar with, using that tried-and-true Arabian venue, storytelling. She loved it! How do I know? The next time we saw her she skittered over to us with a big smile on her face and welcomed each one of us with *both* of her *bare* hands!

Has Amira ever said that she is a believer in Jesus the

Messiah? Not that I know of. Does that discourage us?
Not in the least. There is still a great fear of reprisal among
Muslims, which keeps them from being very open about
their faith. That doesn't mean they don't have faith—however
new, small, or untested.

Once I asked God for a sign that He was working in the
lives of our neighbors. Our family had been away from Little
Town for an extended period, and when we returned things
seemed to have regressed spiritually. Had they forgotten the
things they'd heard and seen of Jesus Christ? Had the evil one
snatched away the seeds sown on this soil? Personally, I was
in need of some encouragement.

I asked the Lord to give me a sign that He was still at work
in our neighbors' hearts by having them serve a special fried
doughball called *luqimaat*. Normally prepared for festive
occasions like weddings or the feasts of Ramadan, it would
be unusual to see it served now. Calling ahead of time,
I arranged to make three visits to old friends one evening.
They were all eager to see our new baby, and I mentioned
that my visits would have to be short since the little one
wouldn't be up to hours of shuffling about. Before leaving,
I asked the Lord if I should bring any materials. A few items
came to mind, which I put into a separate bag and tucked
into the car for safekeeping.

At the first house I had a lovely visit, and the ladies

accepted the gift of a new Gospel film. It was a touching movie focusing on Christ's interaction with women in Scripture—illustrating the way He treated them and the miracles He did for them—demonstrating God's loving care and esteem for the women He created. Shareen, who had been the head of this home since her husband died a few years earlier, liked to extend her authority over me as well. "Before you go home, you will visit Rahma," she informed me.

Rahma had been a dear friend of Shareen's for years, but I didn't really know her very well. We'd met during visits a couple of times, and I had observed her sweet and gentle spirit. When Shareen was healed of an ailment, she'd brought me to Rahma's to pray for one of her afflicted children. Rahma had married at the age of thirteen, and her union with a first cousin had had its effect on their nine offsprings' DNA. One-year-old Fuad had been born with literally half a brain. Lying on the mat, he was clearly small for his age. Although his eyes were open and he appeared to be looking around, his body was limp, flopping like a rag doll when picked up. In the past, three of us believers had prayed over him together, but seemingly to no avail.

I knew that Rahma's house was nearby, but why did I have to make an extra stop there to visit her privately? Why couldn't she just join in at one of the two other houses where I already had appointments?

"Shareen, I still have two more visits to make, and the baby is already getting cranky. Can't you pass my greetings on to Rahma for me?"

At the next house, I was warmly greeted by all of the women except for one—the woman I call "my Arab mother." In fact, she seemed to be rather brusque toward everybody that evening.

"Ya Ummi," I asked, "why aren't you glad to see me?"

Quickly she apologized, "It's this pain in my head! I have such a pain in my head." After asking her some questions about the cause and duration of her problem, as well as what sort of remedies she'd tried, it occurred to me that this was a perfect opportunity to turn the conversation to spiritual things.

"Do you want me to pray for you? Maybe God will remove the pain."

Readily she agreed. There was one new daughter-in-law in the house who had never seen this done before, but the rest of the family had previous

"Do you want me to pray for you? Maybe God will remove the pain." Readily she agreed.

personal experience with how God can answer prayer. That being the case, it bothered me all the more to see them so dull and seemingly unaffected now. Wanting to jog their memories, I prayed out loud, "Oh God in Heaven, I thank You for all the things You have done for this family. You have shown them your love and mercy through answered prayer in the past. You brought them Your Word, and confirmed it to them personally in many ways. Please don't let them forget all You've done for them and all that You have taught them about Yourself and Your ways. Show them again that Jesus is the One Way to You and that You are both willing and able to save them, physically and spiritually. I pray that You will heal my Arab mother of this pain and use that to remind and convince the entire family of all the Truth You have revealed to them. In Jesus' name, Amen."

They, too, accepted a copy of the Gospel film. I can imagine that, after I left, the new daughter-in-law had a lot of questions for her relatives—"What was that woman talking about? What did our family see God do in the past?"

Emerging from the gate in their wall, I saw Rahma running down the street toward me. "You must visit me. Did Shareen tell you? You must come to my house." Explaining that I still had one more appointment to keep, I said I would try to stop by afterwards—although the baby was already exhausted. Why couldn't we just arrange to get together some other time?

At the third house, women I'd arranged to see had been called away. The two who were left to look after the house welcomed me in, but the visit was brief and I left a little early. Immediately, Shareen appeared on the scene again. "Now you will visit Rahma. Come." She didn't seem to notice that the baby was crying loudly and about to come unglued. It was now almost the dinner hour, well past her bedtime. Silently I asked God what to do. *Should I take care of my child or take time for Rahma?* It seemed as if God was saying, *I'll take care of your child. Go see Rahma.*

As soon as I got there, the last prayer call of the day sounded. Everyone scattered, leaving me alone with my howling infant. *Great,* I thought. *How long is this going to take?* Taking God up on His child-care offer, I turned my mind to the opportunity at hand and began to pray. The baby quieted down in just a few minutes. Soon people started coming back into the room, and when I turned around there was a large tray of food on the floor. On it was a whole platter of luscious *luqimaat!* Perhaps I was distracted by the circumstances because, unbelievably, it didn't register that God had just given me the sign I had asked for: He was still at work in the life of my neighbors. He was at work in Rahma's house.

Shareen seemed very pleased with herself as she sat down beside me at the tray. Some of the children came to greet me, and then Rahma brought in Fuad and sat him down in front of us. Fuad *sat*! He was *sitting*!

"He can sit!" My amazement brought proud smiles to the

face of every family member in the room. "What happened? What did you do? This is wonderful!"

An answer burst out of Shareen's mouth before anyone else had a chance to speak. "The doctors told her there was nothing they could do, and that is when Rahma did it herself." She was glorying in her friend's accomplishment, and rightly so. Then Rahma described the daily therapy she faithfully performed for perhaps a year, exercising Fuad's muscles for him until he was able to sit on his own. I showered her with praise. It was an incredible feat, especially with eight other children to tend to and no household help! What love she had for her little son, what patience and faithfulness, God bless her.

Later, when I arose to begin the farewells, Rahma thanked me for coming and shyly added, "Don't you have something for me?" Since it is customary to bring a little bag of fruit or other small gift when visiting someone you haven't seen in a while, I assumed she was referring to that.

"I'm so sorry, but I didn't know I'd be coming here today so I didn't bring anything."

"No, I mean, don't you have something for me?"

Still clueless, I could only ask, "Like what?"

"Well, you gave Shareen a movie . . ."

How big of a hint did she have to give me, for Pete's sake? Did she have to come right out and say, "Please give me Christian materials"?

Finally, I realized what was going on. Shareen had insisted I see Rahma privately in her home, not in order to see Fuad sit, but because Rahma was a seeker! She wanted to hear the Christian message, and Shareen knew I could help her.

At that moment I also realized what dear, close friends these two must be. One was a seeker, yet she trusted her friend enough to share that potentially deadly secret. The other was a committed Muslim, yet she was willing to connect her searching friend to a Christian who might be able to answer her questions. If this were discovered, both women would be equally incriminated.

One was a seeker, yet she trusted her friend enough to share that potentially deadly secret. The other was a committed Muslim, yet she was willing to connect her searching friend to a Christian.

"Yes, I did give Shareen a movie. Do you have a DVD player to watch movies on too?" She didn't, but the Lord had already provided for her specific need. Remembering the items I'd felt prompted to bring, I went out to the car to retrieve them. There was a twelve-volume set of the dramatized Bible on tape, a book called *Journey of Light* written by a former Muslim especially for Muslims, and a cassette of indigenous Arabic praise and worship music. Thanking me repeatedly, Rahma cradled them in her arms, hugging her new treasures to her bosom. Smiling, Shareen nodded her approval and abruptly ended the meeting. "Let's go."

It wasn't until I was in the car and driving away that the whole picture came together. On all of my preplanned visits I had "done ministry," and that was fine. But it was the unplanned, unwanted, seemingly unnecessary visit I wasn't expecting to go on that turned out to be the place God was most at work. I was so thankful that He had not let me miss it.

✛

Have I not commanded you?
Be strong and of good courage;
do not be afraid, nor be dismayed,
for the LORD your God is with
you wherever you go.

JOSHUA 1:9

CHAPTER 5

Family Matters

"What about your children?"

That is probably the question Mike and I are most frequently asked when people learn that we live inside the Arab Muslim World. Our Western friends back home wonder how we can safely raise our children in a place where Islamic fundamentalists also reside. On the other hand, our Eastern neighbors wonder why we didn't move here sooner. When the residents of Little Town discovered that Mike was born and raised in New York, they nodded and smiled knowingly—that's why the American had come to Arabia. He had to get his family away from all those drugs, gangs, prostitutes, mobsters, and muggers!

Of course, there is no place on earth that is truly "safe" from all evil. There are good and bad people everywhere, as well as pros and cons for every living situation. One of the advantages of living here is the minimal exposure our children have had to pornographic images. Male and female bodies that we pass on the street are thoroughly clothed, the advertisements are "clean," and until recently there was even censorship of imported reading materials and movies. After purchasing a foreign magazine or newspaper, it would not be unusual to find that suggestive photos and ads had been blacked out with heavy ink. No doubt sexual sin is as rampant here as it is anywhere, but it is kept hidden rather than enticingly flaunted "in your face."

Our Western friends back home wonder how we can safely raise our children in a place where Islamic fundamentalists also reside. Our Eastern neighbors wonder why we didn't move here sooner.

As most of our Western friends imagine, one disadvantage to living here has been the unavailability of so many things that can make life "nicer" and more like home. This was much more true during our first few years in Arabia than it is now. Oh, to have had an ant trap that actually killed ants. A household cleanser that actually smelled clean. Or shoes that fit our supersized American feet. Paper towels, ice cube trays, a whistling teakettle. Vicks VapoRub, ChapStick, Nestlé chocolate chips. The pain, of course, is in knowing that exactly what you want is, at this very moment, sitting on the third shelf from the bottom in aisle 5 of your hometown's Walmart superstore. It could be yours for less than five bucks if it weren't on the other side of Earth.

Though unworthy to be mentioned alongside greater concerns such as religious oppression or the trampling of human rights, these things, small as they are, somehow matter in the day-to-day business of living.

No matter where families may live, parents will be praying for their children's safety, for their character development, and for their future.

In any location, whatever the pros and cons may be, one thing is for sure. Our kids have to learn to know and trust God, just like your kids do. Just like you and I do too. No matter where families may live, parents will be praying for their children's safety, for their character development, and for their future. In this chapter, I'd like to shift gears for a moment and share just a little of how God has been faithful to our family within the setting He has chosen for us.

When Mike and I came to Arabia, we knew that God had led us here. It had been relatively easy for us to leave the familiarity of our home country, in anticipation of what God had in store. But what about Tim? When I carried him on our first venture into the local *souq* (market), he clutched at my blouse in fear of the black-robed figures filling the streets. Burying his face in my bosom, his alarmed little voice was muffled into my clothing, "Mom, look! Witches!" Of course, explaining that the mommies in Arabia wear black covers to be modest was just the beginning. How would the Lord ever make this strange place "home" for our family?

In the early days, we temporarily lived in a tiny apartment building that housed three families with children, one single person, and the maintenance man with his widowed mother. One family's son, Muhammad, was just a year or two older than our five-year-old, Tim, and those boys hit it off right from the start. Still, it was an act of faith for Mike and me the first time we allowed our little guy to go play at Muhammad's house all by himself. I was thankful that for some reason they normally played in our flat or outside where I could watch them from the balcony.

One particular day, I noticed that Tim was quite absorbed in wrapping up a number of his toys in notebook paper and taping them like gifts. After he'd prepared an armload full of these "presents," he tried to duck out the front door without my noticing. Head down, he mumbled, "Bye, Mom. I'll see you later."

"Whoa, wait a minute there, partner. Where do you think you're going, and why do you have those toys all wrapped up?"

"I wrapped these for Muhammad." He paused before going on. "I'm giving them to him for a present." It was apparent Tim was expecting me to disapprove. Fearing that his plans might be foiled, he quickly stated his case. "Mom, you should see his house. All his brothers and sisters and him only have one toy and one plastic horse to play with, and both of them are broken. I have lots of toys, so I want to give these to Muhammad. They're mine, so I can give 'em to somebody if I want to, right?"

At that moment, arms piled high with toys of sacrifice, our son looked like the poster child for a "What Would Jesus Do?" campaign. I could imagine his guardian angel standing behind him, along with the cloud of witnesses, staring down at me as if to say, "You're not going to blow this, are you?"

Arms piled high with toys of sacrifice, our son looked like the poster child for a "What Would Jesus Do?" campaign.

Naturally, I responded by saying, "Sure you can, Tim. They are your toys, and I'm proud of you for sharing with your friend."

Then another part of me, the part that was thinking, *What on earth are you doing? Don't you know we are living on a missionary income?* piped up. It was important that the boy realize his sacrifice really was going to be *his* sacrifice, not an easy giveaway subsidized by Mom and Dad. That part of me just had to add, "But hey, don't give any more toys away or you won't have anything left to play with at home, okay? Dad and I can't be buying toys to replace what you give away."

Tim was unfazed after counting the cost. His bright little face seemed to grow a few watts brighter with the parental blessing upon his mission, and he hurried off to deliver his presents. I wondered how they would be received, wrapped up in the crumpled notebook paper and all. Maybe Muhammad's family would misunderstand and be offended. Even worse, what if they offended Tim in response? His gesture was one of sincere friendship and goodwill.

A while later Tim returned. His face was beaming, and he had a flower in his hand. Holding it up like a precious

It was more than just a flower to Tim. It was Muhammad's sincere gesture of friendship.

treasure, he announced, "Muhammad really liked the toys. He went outside and walked all over until he found a bush with flowers on it that he could reach. Then he climbed up and picked this and gave it to me for a present! Can I have a glass of water for it, Mom?" It was more than just a flower to Tim. It was Muhammad's sincere gesture of friendship. That flower stayed in the place of honor on Tim's bedside table well past its expiration.

God knew our son and had provided the very thing he needed most in order to make Arabia "home" for him. God had given him a friend. Who would have thought Tim's loving response to the need of relative strangers would result in his own most significant need being met? Mike and I never cease to be amazed by, and to learn from, our heavenly Father's parenting. His workings in our children's lives have been a witness of their own to those around us.

✝ ✝ ✝

On the way out of Little Town to do some errands one morning, seven-year-old Tim was sitting in the front seat of the car. He was unusually quiet and thoughtful as I drove down the dusty street. Breaking the silence, he decided to voice the concerns that were weighing on his young mind. "Mom, are we going to live in Little Town forever?"

The negative tone of the question surprised me since Tim had always been happy with his life here. He'd never known any other home. When we left the States, Tim had been less than three years old. Those first few years of his life had been spent traveling to hundreds of churches to share our vision and establish a support base. Our house in Little Town was the very first home we'd had as a family. Getting down to the reason for his question, I asked, "Why? Don't you want to live here forever?"

With the kind of soberness that comes from having thoroughly examined an idea from all sides, he admitted, "I want to live in America sometimes because it snows there and it never snows here. The kids in America get to play in the snow every day."

Tim's answer was a relief. And cute. I was glad to know we weren't facing a major crisis. However, I also knew that no amount of global warming was going to make it snow in our desert. Trying to sound encouraging, I reminded my child that although it couldn't snow in a place like this, it did rain here in the winter, and rain is fun too.

"But we had winter, and it didn't rain," he lamented.

Unfortunately, he was right. The fact was that it hadn't rained for the past three winters. The concept that God must have a good reason for not making it rain and that there was probably some great higher purpose did little to satisfy his boyish yearnings. Giving up my lame attempts at reason, I tried to cheer Tim up by talking about what he wanted to do the next time it did rain. He promptly rattled off a whole list of ideas for playing in the rain. It was obvious he'd been pondering this weather subject for some time. As he was talking, a lightbulb clicked on somewhere in Tim's mind. He had a brilliant idea!

"You know, Mom, God could make it rain in the summer. He can make it rain whenever He wants to."

Immediately I knew where his line of thinking was headed. *Oh no!* I thought. *Lord, don't let this kid pray for rain.* Let me confess right here, I didn't believe God would send rain. First of all, the weathermen here don't even have to get out of bed in the morning. There's nothing for them to forecast. Every day it's "hot, sunny, and clear," and in the summer it's "hotter, sunnier, and clearer." Second, we were in the middle of a three-year drought. Third, it was August—the hottest, driest time of the calendar year. Sure, God can do anything, but He wasn't going to suddenly make it rain right out of the (literally) clear, blue sky. I couldn't imagine how our young son would ever take such a hit to his faith.

Immediately I knew where his line of thinking was headed. Oh no! *I thought.* Lord, don't let this kid pray for rain.

But he grew bolder as he went on, "God can make it rain right now. I think we should ask Him. Let's pray."

Before I could say anything, Tim's small hand was firmly gripping mine, and his head was bowed in prayer. "Dear God, if it would please You, and if it won't mess up any of Your other plans, could You please make it rain? We'll understand if there's some reason You don't want it to rain right now, but if it would be okay, we'd really like some rain . . ."

The next day was a normal summer day. Our window-unit

air conditioners were managing to keep the house at around 85 to 90 degrees, which was at least 30 degrees below the outdoor temperature. Tim was playing alone in his room while Lydia napped, and I was in the middle of vacuuming the living room. As often happens in the summer months, the electricity cut out. With the roaring and rattling of all the machines silenced, the house grew very still—and very hot—very quickly. Not knowing how long the outage would last, I lay down on the carpet to rest from the heat until the immobilized machinery would be able to start up again. Because of the interruption to our activity and the intense quiet, Tim and I gradually became aware of a sound outside. It was a kind of rumbling sound.

Tim mentioned it first. "Mom, do you hear that?"

It sounded like thunder, but of course it wasn't. "It must be a plane," I answered. The rumbling sound swelled again. "No," I admitted, "that couldn't be a plane. Let's go look."

Opening the front door, I was surprised at how dark it was outside. It was just about noon, but it looked as if the sun had almost set. Unable to see the sky because of the porch roof, which extended fourteen feet outward from the house, we had to go all the way out into the yard in order to look up and see what was going on.

There, poised directly above our house, was the darkest, densest rain cloud I have ever seen. Hanging unusually low, it looked as if it had been pulled down out of the sky by the burden of its own immense weight. About two city blocks in size, as best I could guess from where I stood beneath it, the cloud was perfectly centered above our home. Tim and I stood there looking up, mouths gaping. Then we heard another sound. It was the *plink! plink! plink!* of raindrops beginning to fall onto our corrugated metal carport.

"Tim! God is answering your prayer! Do you feel the raindrops? It's actually raining!"

Tim put his hands on his hips and surveyed the situation. "Actually, I was expecting more rain than this." Resolved to make the most of it anyway, he turned to go in and get his umbrella. As soon as he did, the cloud broke. It was a full-fledged downpour.

Our neighbors emerged from their houses and stood in the rain, undeterred by the soaking. Looking up at the spectacle, they marveled to one another, "What is this? How can this be?" Children came out of the woodwork and into the streets to play in the cooling rain. Tim got to do everything on his what-he-would-do-if-it-rained list and then came inside to ask me for a cup of hot cocoa. ("Because," he explained, "that's what kids in America do after they play in the rain.") When he was finished, the rain stopped.

Sometimes I wonder: What if Tim had prayed for snow?

✣ ✣ ✣

Our family had been a part of Little Town for several years now and had seen God work over and over, giving us opportunities to share His Word and then confirming it to people's hearts. Muslims were hearing the Gospel. Some had received Bibles, literature, videos, or cassette tapes. Mike had led one Muslim man to Christ and discipled another. But now it seemed that the enemy was retaliating for his losses.

Muslims were hearing the Gospel. But now it seemed that the enemy was retaliating for his losses.

Our second child, four-year-old Lydia, was having frequent nightmares. We had tried everything we knew to relieve her of them. After our family prayers, we all said an extra prayer for Lydia. We quoted Scriptures and asked God to protect her and give her good dreams. Pertinent verses were chosen from the Bible for our little one to memorize and claim. We taught her how to pray by herself more specifically. Sometimes it seemed to help, but many times it didn't. Why the inconsistency? For all our prayers and efforts, she was waking up terrified three or four times a night. Rushing into our room, she would jump into bed between Mike and me, where she felt safe. Then, after pouring out all her scary experiences and receiving comfort from Mom and Dad, she'd finally fall back to sleep. Unfortunately, *I* couldn't sleep with Lydia in the bed. Lying awake on my edge of the mattress, I'd wait for the moment when her sleep was deep enough for me to pick her up, carry her to her own room, and tuck her in. Just as I got back to sleep myself, Lydia would awaken with another nightmare and the cycle would be repeated. I was dragging out of bed exhausted, morning after morning, for weeks. The nightmares affected our whole family and were rendering me dysfunctional for everyday life, let alone ministry.

To top it off, our neighbors were observing this whole thing and scolding us about it. In their thinking, it wasn't even safe for an adult to sleep alone at night. When they went to bed, all the females slept together in one room and all the males in another. In addition, each room had a *jinn* light and all the children wore amulets to ward off evil. They even dressed baby boys as girls, hoping the evil spirits would mistake them for worthless females and not bother to harm them. They marveled at our thickheadedness. Why did we invest so much effort in prayer, expecting God to protect our children, when we weren't even willing to use a simple amulet? Did we think God had nothing better to do than take care of our children for us? How preposterous to imagine He would concern Himself with such trivia.

While we were putting the children to bed one night, I reached the end of my rope. As usual, Lydia had been pleading for Mommy to stay with her until she fell asleep. Tired beyond sympathy, I said, "Lydia, honey, look. Mommy can't go to bed with you at seven thirty every night. We have prayed for you, your door is open, your light is on, and you can even see your big brother from your bed. There is nothing else I can do for you. Jesus is the only one who can do anything more, so you'll just have to ask *Him* to help you." Lydia became silent and sullen as I turned and left the room.

As soon as I walked out that door, the pangs of guilt and remorse hit. What kind of mother was I, leaving a frightened child in bed alone? On the other hand, how much could a parent take? And wasn't this actually God's fault—where was He in all of this? Here we were doing everything we knew to trust in Him, and He seemed to be ignoring our cries for help. Completely drained physically, mentally, emotionally, and spiritually, I melted into bed.

As soon as I walked out that door, the pangs of guilt and remorse hit. And wasn't this actually God's fault—where was He in all of this?

When I awoke it was morning. Morning! Where was Lydia? She hadn't come in all night. Had she been afraid to come for help after what I'd said? Had she spent the whole night in fear with no one to run to, no one to comfort her? Leaping out of bed,

I ran to her room. There she was, sound asleep and looking as peaceful as an angel.

Some time later, the padding of small feet on the carpet announced that Lydia was up. Pulling her onto my lap for a good morning kiss, I asked the question I'd been waiting all morning to ask.

"Honey, you didn't come into Mommy and Daddy's bed last night. Didn't you have any scary dreams?"

"Yes, I did have a scary dream," she answered in a cheerful voice. She was smiling; her face and body were relaxed. "I asked Daddy Jesus for help like you told me to." (Lydia never said "Jesus," she always said "Daddy Jesus.")

That was it? She just asked Daddy Jesus for help and went back to sleep? That explanation seemed a little too easy after weeks and weeks of unrelenting fear. I probed further, "Okay. And how did Jesus help you?"

"Well, when I got scared I called Him and He came in my room. Then He sat on my bed and rubbed my back and sang me a song."

"You mean you dreamed He did that?"

"No, He came in there," her chubby little finger pointed to the door, "and He sat on my bed right here. And He rubbed my back, just like you do, and sang me a song."

"What kind of song?"

"He sang me a song about He loves me," she replied sweetly.

Her beaming face confirmed that whatever God had done in answer to this little one's cry for help, and however He had done it, it had certainly driven away all fear.

Her beaming face confirmed that whatever God had done in answer to this little one's cry for help, and however He had done it, it had certainly driven away all fear.

Just to satisfy my own curiosity, I couldn't resist asking one more question, "Um, Lydia, what did Daddy Jesus look like?"

Flipping through the mental files of her four-year-old vocabulary list, her eyes brightened as she hit upon just the right description. Excitedly she explained, "He looked—He looked like Daddy Jesus!"

From that day on there were no more nightmares or sleepless nights. What's more, good fruit was born in Lydia's life as she began to comfort others with the same comfort she had received from God. Anytime she saw other children crying, hurt, or fearful, she would rush to their side and reassure them with the greatest words of encouragement she knew, "Don't worry. Daddy Jesus is here, and He loves you!"

✢

Then the seventy returned with joy, saying, "Lord, even the demons are subject to us in Your name."

LUKE 10:17

CHAPTER 6

The *Jinn* and the Evil Eye

Quiet times were getting pretty predictable. The same idea kept coming to mind during almost every season of private prayer. It seemed God was telling me to pray for a "Mount Carmel experience" in our neighbor-hood. Something that would dem-onstrate the emptiness and futility of Islam and showcase the reality that Jesus Christ is Lord. Although I didn't know what sort of circumstances God might engineer to bring that about, I'd been praying for it for over a year now. Mike and I were beginning to wonder if God was ever going to actually do it.

It seemed God was telling me to pray for a "Mount Carmel experience" in our neighborhood. Something that would showcase the reality that Jesus Christ is Lord.

A few months before we were due

to take an extended trip out of the country, Amal invited "the gals" over for an evening visit at her apartment. Amal was a single Arab businesswoman and a keen believer. "The gals" consisted of three women from Mozi's family, Amal's new Western roommate, and myself. It fell to me to be the chauffeur.

In full accordance with some unwritten law of Arab culture, Mozi wasn't ready on time when I came to pick them up. Going inside to wait in the *majlis*, I was struck by the bizarre appearance of Dini—or was it Hilma? It had always been impossible for me to tell the twins apart—until they opened their mouths, that is. Eighteen-year-old Dini was usually discreet, quiet, and concerned with religious appearance, while her identical twin, Hilma, would probably have been a Spice Girl if she'd grown up in the West. The diametric apposition of their personalities was a natural subject of playful humor. But there was nothing playful or humorous in the atmosphere at their house tonight. Dini was as rigid as a board and seemed to be in a trance, as if she were some kind of living statue. She didn't even appear to be aware that I had entered the room. She didn't appear to be aware, period. Her grandmother came in and began to scold and beat the oblivious teenager in front of me, finally dragging her off to another room. Just as they went out, another door opened and a disheveled Hilma entered. Sitting down brusquely against a wall, Hilma immediately fell into the same stoic statue pose of her sister. She, too, seemed unaware of my presence, and the blank stare was eerie. Without any warning at all, she burst into harsh, cackling, freakish laughter. Just as instantaneously she stopped, her features frozen back into a face of stone. Bizarre is putting it mildly.

At last, Mozi had herself ready to go. Needless to say, Dini and Hilma weren't coming. As the two of us drove off, I just had to know what was wrong with the girls.

"Have they been trying drugs?"

My friend was appalled at the suggestion. "Reema! You know they would never do anything like that. They're good girls. It's not drugs; it's the *jinn*."

Depending on whom you ask, you'll get different definitions of exactly what *jinn* are supposed to be. Mozi meant evil spirits. She explained that the grandmother of the twins had been boasting about their good grades at one of the morning visit groups. A neighbor there had been shamed by this because her own son was doing miserably in school. The story was that this jealous woman had cast the "evil eye" on Dini and Hilma. Although there are incantations and spells that can be used when one has an earnest desire for bad things to befall someone else, the evil eye is most often given in the form of a compliment during ordinary conversation. If you compliment an Arab Muslim, you have actually

WHICH NONE CAN SHUT

cursed him unless you follow your compliment with the phrase "*ma sha' allah.*" It's considered a curse because drawing attention to someone's blessing or good fortune, in effect, invites the *jinn* to come and take it away. Saying the words "what Allah has willed" invokes Allah to protect and preserve whatever was complimented.

To my surprise, this problem at Mozi's house had been going on for some time. The family had been carefully guarding its shameful secret by keeping the girls locked up inside the house. Seeking a cure, they had consulted the local religious teachers/medicine men in earnest. In three months' time, they had put their teenage daughters through thousands of dollars' worth of treatments at the hands of seven different *mutawwa*s.

Seeking a cure, they had consulted the local religious teachers/medicine men in earnest.

"What do you mean 'treatments'? What did they actually do?" I asked Mozi.

"Different things. They told us to hire people to read the Quran out loud in our home all day and all night, around the clock. And sometimes they made the girls drink tea with a verse from the Quran dissolved in it. The *jinn* are supposed to fly out when they hear or see the words of God."

"Did it work?"

"No. Another time there was a special drink to make them

vomit. When they threw up the poison, the *jinn* were supposed to come out too."

"Did that do anything?"

"No, but the *mutawwa*s have many methods. They also strangled them."

"*What?!*"

"Not to kill them, to help them. They would squeeze their necks until they fell to the ground lifeless. That way the *jinn* would think they were dead and leave them."

"And?"

"So far, nothing has helped."

As soon as that news reached my ears, a light went on in my head. Immediately I knew. This was the Mount Carmel experience I'd been praying a whole year for! Mozi's family had spent all that time, all that money, going to all those Islamic authorities and got *nothing* as a result. Nothing Islam had to offer could meet their need. It was empty and futile! I could almost see the silver platter as God finally presented the opportunity we'd been waiting for—the opportunity to see the Father exalt His Son in the sight of our friends and neighbors, testifying to them of His ability and willingness to save them through Christ.

"Mozi, I am so sorry that Dini and Hilma are going through all of this. But I'm so happy because I know what to do about it!" She was unconvinced, to say the least. After all, my family was the neighborhood project, remember? And this was a dilemma that even their religious experts had not been able to crack.

"Oh, Reema," she said, half-smiling at my naive optimism. "What could you know about this kind of thing?"

"Well, it's not that I know anything. But God does, and in His Word He's given us everything we need to know for this life. Who made the *jinn*?"

"Allah, of course."

"Right, so who do you need to help you if you want the *jinn* to leave you alone?"

"Allah."

"Right. So did you pray and ask God to get rid of the *jinn* for you?"

Picture an eye roll here. "Of *course* we did."

"Of course you did," I repeated. "And it didn't work, did it?"

"No . . ." At this point it was probably sheer curiosity (rather than hope) that held Mozi's attention.

Nearly bursting with joy, I continued, "You prayed, God didn't answer, and I know why." I felt myself beaming. A whole year of prayer. There was no way God wasn't going to do this. It was Mount Carmel.

"Well . . . why?"

"It's because all authority in Heaven, and on earth, and under the earth has been given to the Lord Jesus Christ. No one comes to the Father except through Him. Did you go through Jesus when you prayed to God?"

"You know we can't do that; we're Muslims."

"Right, and your prayers didn't work. But I can pray for you in Jesus' name because I'm a Christian. I believe that if you let me pray for the twins, they'll be healed. God's Word promises that if His children ask anything in Jesus' name, He will hear and answer them. He doesn't answer our prayers because we are anything, but because of who Jesus is." At that moment, we pulled up in front of Amal's apartment building. Mozi needed time to think about this, so we agreed to talk more later.

It turned out that a few other ladies had been invited to the visit as well. We enjoyed the company and the generous spread that Amal and her roommate had prepared for us. I was glad for our hostesses' sake that the additional guests were there to help put a dent in the refreshments, since Dini and Hilma hadn't been able to come. When it was nearly time to go, most of the ladies were occupied in another room looking at photo albums, so Amal, Mozi, and I found ourselves alone in the *majlis*. Mozi was just as close to Amal as she was to me and decided to take this private opportunity to share her sisters' predicament, and our conversation in the car, with her.

"So Reema says that all you Christians have to do is pray

in Jesus' name and God will remove the *jinn*. Is that true?" She clearly respected the opinion of her educated and accomplished fellow Arab.

Amal thought for a moment before responding, "Yes, that's true."

Mozi stared at her two Christian friends in disbelief. The next thought to cross Mozi's mind visibly appeared on her face. The look in her eyes, the wry smile—it was like watching a chess player who suddenly realizes her next move will result in a victorious "checkmate." She would *let* her Christian friends pray, and nothing would happen. After all, how could it? Although the twins would still have the *jinn*, they wouldn't be any worse off than they were now and all our biblical claims about Jesus would be categorically discredited, once and for all. This single failed prayer would effectively silence our Christian witness in the neighborhood forever.

She would let *her Christian friends pray, and nothing would happen. After all, how could it? Between Islam and Jesus, the stage was now set.*

Between Islam and Jesus, the stage was now set.

"So what do you have to do to make this prayer? Kill a chicken? Burn incense?"

Amal and I consulted with each other, calling to mind pertinent verses from God's Word. "No, we just have to ask in Jesus' name. Since Jesus' death and resurrection is what removes our uncleanness and makes us acceptable in God's sight, it's only through Him that we can approach the holy Lord of the universe."

"Okay," Mozi brushed the explanation aside, "you can pray for Dini and Hilma."

"Do you want to call your parents and get permission from your family first?" We didn't want to be accused later of anything that might seem to tarnish the glory God was about to receive in this heavenly contest. It had to be done properly, above reproach.

"No," Mozi was confident she didn't need permission for something that wasn't going to happen. "Go ahead."

The two of us bowed our heads and prayed, "Oh God our Father, we praise You! You are above all things because You made all things. We give thanks that You know us, love us, and care about every detail of our lives. You love Dini, Hilma, and their whole family and desire for them to know and love You too. In the name of the Lord Jesus Christ, please remove the *jinn* from these two young women and heal them completely. We specifically ask that You heal them right now while we are praying, so that it will be clear that their deliverance was Your answer to this prayer given in Jesus' name, not as a result of any other cause. And we pray that You will do it in such a way as to show Mozi that Jesus

Christ really is who Your Word says He is, the Lord of all and the only Way to You."

When I dropped Mozi off, she didn't invite me in like she normally did after an outing together. Dying to know how God was effecting His deliverance, I rushed home to tell Mike the news so we could await the outcome together.

Getting the story out of Mozi over the phone the next morning was like pulling teeth. It was obvious she didn't want to tell me what had happened. Practically whining, she drew her sentences out so long it seemed they would snap. "The twins? Oh . . . uh . . . they're . . . well, they're . . . better."

"What do you mean 'better'? How much better? All the way better, a little better, what?"

"Reema . . . what can I say?"

"You can say how the twins are!"

But she wouldn't. On subsequent visits to the house, Dini and Hilma were ushered away as soon as I appeared at the door. Although my relationship with everyone else was apparently the same as ever, they were literally kept in another room until I left. Clearly the family didn't want me asking them any questions. Or were they afraid the girls had questions for me? One thing was for sure, nobody was gloating about how the prayer in Jesus' name hadn't worked. Had Mozi even told them? All attempts to ask the family what had happened were greeted with a change of subject.

Finally the time came for my family to take our trip out of the country. There had been a long-standing pact between me and the eight women of Mozi's household—that we would somehow get permission from the men to go to Big Town Restaurant all by ourselves before I left. Permission had been granted, and there I was, waiting with the car as usual until the ladies were finally ready to go. That farewell was made especially memorable when Dini and Hilma were allowed to come! True to their natures, Dini declined our excursion out into the mixed company of a public restaurant at the last moment, and Hilma dressed in red (even though she had to wear a black head-to-toe covering on top of it!). The two of them couldn't have been more their normal selves than that. I knew then in my heart that they'd been delivered from the *jinn*, but no one in their family knew how to cope with what that meant.

It was unthinkable to them that Islam could be wrong. The very idea rocked the foundations of the entire world they lived in.

Naturally, it was unthinkable to them that Islam could be wrong. The very idea rocked the foundations of the entire world they lived in. Every aspect of their personal and public life was governed by it, their whole society was built on it, their history gloried in it. Mozi's family, like every other family in the neighborhood, had always lived according to prescribed Islamic methods, as had their ancestors. They prayed in the Muslim prayer positions at the time of the Muslim prayer calls. They ate what a Muslim should eat in the way a Muslim should eat it. They washed themselves as a Muslim should wash, dressed as a Muslim should dress, celebrated as a Muslim should celebrate, and mourned as a Muslim should mourn. But if Jesus is Lord . . . then what? How did followers of Jesus wash? When and what did they pray? If a Muslim became a follower of Jesus, how was he supposed to eat his next meal? What overwhelming complications being a Muslim seemed to attach to the simple command of Elijah on Mount Carmel, "If the LORD is God, follow Him" (1 Kings 18:21). Apparently the family had decided that the only way to cope, for now, was denial.

When we returned from dinner, it was time to say good-bye. It would be more than a year before we could hope to see each other again. The nine of us stood near the door for a long time reminiscing, talking, hugging, and wiping away tears. Dini and Hilma pulled me away from all the hubbub for a moment, taking my hands in theirs and pulling me close. "Reema, while you are gone . . . pray for us every day."

Why were they asking me that? Did they know about the prayer at Amal's house? Searching them out, I reminded them why Christian prayers are considered *haraam*, a shame and offense against God: "When I pray, I pray in Jesus' name."

They squeezed my hands tighter, "*We know.* Pray for us, every day." Just then we were intercepted, and I had to say the final farewell with so many questions still unanswered.

Some time later, while we were in the States, I called to check in on Mozi and the twins.

"Hallo?" She sounded as if she were right next door.

"Hi, Mozi! It's me, Reema."

"Reema!" Her happiness radiated across the phone lines, "Jesus is good!"

The greeting floored me. "W-what did you say?"

My Arab friend was all atwitter with excitement as she went on to explain the good news. "Dini and Hilma were able to go back and finish school. They will graduate! Dini is even going on to university. Jesus is good!"

At last she had given glory to the Lord Jesus Christ with her own lips! She had credited Him for the deliverance of her two sisters who had been held under the power of evil spirits, a power that nothing in Islam had been able to free them from. What Mike, Amal, and I had believed by faith was now confirmed by Mozi's testimony.

✢ ✢ ✢

Almost three years later, God offered us a glimpse of His work within the soul of Mozi's family. It came through a telling conversation with Jamila, the mother of Hamdan, who had also raised granddaughters Dini and Hilma as her own. Even though nothing had appeared to be happening on the surface, things must have begun adding up for Jamila. She had a veritable "witness list" of experiences, all testifying for the Lord Jesus Christ: the Truth she'd heard during spiritual conversations with her two Christian friends; the *mutawwas'* failed efforts to expel the *jinn* from her granddaughters, and their consequent deliverance in Jesus' name; the apparent backfiring of the SIA plan, and the dramatic change in Hamdan.

In a neighborhood full of very large families who do everything in community, it was rare to have a conversation alone with anyone. That day, Jamila and I spoke privately for only the second time in our lives. The first time had been briefly on the night of the SIA setup. How different the atmosphere in the room was now.

"This Quran is doing nothing for us. I want to hear your Book."

We had all been sobered and saddened by the recent tragic death of Hilma at age twenty-one. It was in the somber and reflective mood of the weeks surrounding her funeral that Jamila had begun listening to the dramatized Bible on tape. That, like so many other things, had come about in an unexpected way. Frustrated that playing audiocassettes of the Quran twenty-four hours a day had not brought healing to Hilma, she'd turned to me and said, "What about your Book? Do you have the Bible on tape? This Quran is doing nothing for us. I want to hear your Book." The way God had been touching her family, and now the words of His Book, were sinking in deeply. As we talked together now, meditations that had been held down in the depths of her heart began to rise up like bubbles, surfacing gently but abruptly into the conversation.

"I can't be like you." *Pop!* Where had that come from?

Startled, my automatic response was to laugh. "Why would you want to be like me? I don't even want to be like me." When she didn't laugh or look up, I realized what she was trying to say. She couldn't be a Christian like me.

"I have to wear *serwals*," she continued. *Serwal*s are long, baggy underwear that start at the waist and reach all the way down to cover the ankles. The ankle portion is fitted very tightly so that it can't ride up, in order to ensure a Muslim woman does not compromise her modesty.

Drawing closer to Jamila and lowering my voice so as not to attract the attention of anyone who might walk by the door, I gently reminded her, "I wear *serwal*s."

Since the day we moved into our home in Little Town, our family had tried to live our Christian life within the confines of our neighbors' Eastern culture, and that had included my wearing the local dress. We wanted to be an example of how they could follow Jesus in their world. (Although we made our share of cultural blunders, everyone was so pleased we were trying to fit in that they quickly forgave us and set us straight.) In the beginning, most of our neighbors wrongly believed that all Westerners were automatically "Christian." Since Muslims identify themselves to a large degree by certain codes of dress, they often assume they must dress like Westerners when they become believers. Thankfully, as they had gotten to know us, many of our neighbors had come to understand the difference between being "from the West" and being "a follower of Christ." Despite all that, the idea of separating ethnic culture from religious practice still seemed an inconquerable hurdle to Jamila. Her religion had built her culture. How could she be an Arab without being Muslim? She needed to think this through.

"I have to wear the *shayla*," my elderly friend continued. It was the covering so gracefully wrapped around her head and thin shoulders. Somehow the way Arab women wear it actually enhances their natural beauty, although meant to cover it. I've never seen a foreigner who could look as lovely in a *shayla* as they do.

"I wear a *shayla* too." My heart and voice filled with sympathy for the struggle she was going through. "Jamila, God is not from the West. He made the whole world—east, west, north, and south. And when Jesus walked the earth, He wore the same kind of clothes your husband wears today. He lived His whole life in the Middle East, like you."

Perhaps that satisfied her, because she left the issue of clothing and turned to traditions. "When my husband dies, I have to sit in a corner." She was referring to the mourning period of a widow, who is required to stay indoors for four months and ten days to demonstrate appropriate grief and respect for her dead spouse, but at that moment I knew it represented all her people's ways.

"Dear Jamila, you don't have to stop being an Arab in order to believe in Jesus. God in Heaven is the God of all human beings, in every country and culture of the earth.

"What I mean is, for example, look at birds. How many kinds did God make? Just one? No, He made hundreds of kinds of birds. Some sing beautifully, some squawk, some can't even fly. But God said that every one of them is good, and each gives glory to Him in its own way. It's the same with all of God's creation, including mankind. Many Arab customs are good. All you need to do is believe with your heart that Jesus is the Way to God. God made you who you are, and He will teach you how to follow

✛

"God made you who you are, and He will teach you how to follow Jesus in your own country, in your own culture, and in your own family. He loves you."

✛

Jesus in your own country, in your own culture, and in your own family. He loves you just as you are, and you can trust Him."

Just then, our conversation was interrupted. There was an argument about something going on in the kitchen, and Jamila was being called on to sort out the scuffle in her domain. As the oldest mother in the house, her word would prevail.

As suddenly as they had emerged, the meditations of Jamila's heart again receded into a secret place, and all was still. At least on the surface. But as she had just revealed, still waters do run deep.

✛

But Peter, standing up with the eleven,
raised his voice and said to them,
"Men of Judea and all who dwell in
Jerusalem, let this be known to you,
and heed my words. For these are not
drunk, as you suppose, since it is only
the third hour of the day. But this is
what was spoken by the prophet Joel:

'And it shall come to pass in
    the last days, says God,
That I will pour out of
    My Spirit on all flesh;
Your sons and your daughters
    shall prophesy,
Your young men shall see visions,
Your old men shall dream dreams. . . .
And it shall come to pass
That whoever calls on the
    name of the LORD
Shall be saved.'"

ACTS 2:14-17, 21

CHAPTER 7

Dreams and Visions

Faisal and his wife, Shareen, had always been devoted
Muslims, performing all of the obligations of Islam faithfully. In addition to doing their ritual prayers, ablutions,
almsgiving, and fasting, they helped build mosques and dig
wells for the poor in hopes of gaining some favor in the eyes
of Allah. Yearly during the month of Ramadan, Shareen still
goes without sleep for three consecutive days and nights in
order to pray. It is said that whatever you are praying for
when the "window of Heaven" opens will be granted to you
by Allah. The problem is that there are so many different
traditions regarding exactly when that window opens. Shareen's particular set of beliefs narrows the possibilities down
to a very specific three-day period. Keeping awake and in
constant prayer for such an extended time is an incredibly

arduous task, yet she is driven by the hope of securing a guaranteed answer to her prayers. That's because, despite all their earnest and sincere efforts to please God, Faisal and Shareen had never been able to find peace, confidence, or assurance about anything in this life. Or the next. The Quran makes no comforting promises for them to rest their faith on.

Has Shareen ever heard the Gospel? Yes, numerous times. Each time, it's as if an invisible barrier suddenly comes up between us, preventing her from grasping the words. She leans forward in earnest, straining to understand. "Tell me again. Tell me again." Yet she is not able to comprehend the gift of eternal life through Christ Jesus. The loving Father God of the Bible is such a foreign concept to her, having tried to appease the impersonal, distant god of Islam all her life.

The loving Father God of the Bible is such a foreign concept to her, having tried to appease the impersonal, distant god of Islam all her life.

When Faisal was diagnosed with cancer, the effects on his entire family were devastating. His illness was long and ended in death, leaving his widow with five of their six children still in school. Shareen had no living relatives to depend on, only an elderly mother who depended on her. Faisal's relatives had made it clear that once he passed away they would not be liable for any kind of financial or material support. Considering the employment potential of an uneducated woman in this society, her family's future seemed pretty bleak.

Shareen had always been proud of what a good husband and father Faisal was. She was going to sorely miss him. One evening, very near the end of Faisal's life on earth, I went to sit and grieve with her. Although I didn't want her to bother with serving refreshments for my visit, custom ruled. Guests had to be honored with trays of far more food and drink than they could possibly consume. Not to do so would be considered an insult to the guest or a great shame on the host. However, the tray Shareen now laid before me held only a bare plate dotted with a few withered dates and a virtually empty coffeepot. I knew this must be all she had left to offer. Of course, I didn't want to take my dear friend's last morsel, yet to refuse her feeble hospitality would have been even worse. Accepting one date, I ate it ever so slowly.

We sat for a time in silence, keenly aware of the life that was gradually slipping away in the next room. The sorrow and fear that had been building in her soul as her husband's condition deteriorated suddenly overflowed in a cry of lament.

"Oh, what shall I do! What shall I do for me, my children, and my old mother?" She began to list all the relatives she had anticipated would draw near to support her family through these terrible circumstances, yet who had actually

WHICH NONE CAN SHUT

done just the opposite. Despairing, she groaned, "Oh, who will take care of us . . . ?" The situation was dire, indeed. Yet there was hope, if my friend could just see it.

"Shareen, none of these people can take care of you and your family forever. Even if they wanted to, they're not rich and they have their own children and aging relatives to provide for. Only God can take care of you and your family's needs every day for the rest of your lives. He made you and He cares about you. Pray and ask Him for help."

"I do pray. I'm a good Muslim. I pray five times a day." But the expression on her face seemed to ask, *What does praying to God have to do with living your life and being able to feed your kids?*

"My friend, you are a good Muslim. And it's good that you pray." The words were meant to be reassuring. It *is* good to pray. But Shareen still needed to know the one true God who answers prayer. "What do you pray for, exactly?"

"Well, after the ritual prayers, I ask God to bless us and do good to us."

"And what good things has He done?"

I could imagine her thinking, *My husband is dying in the next room and you ask how God is blessing me?* But she knew me well enough that she took a moment to consider the question. Somewhere in the darkness that was hanging over Shareen, a light came on.

"Actually, this neighbor over here," she gestured in the direction of a nearby home, "has sent over a tray of cooked rice every day at mealtime."

"That's terrific!" I was thrilled to know about this evidence of God's grace in her life. She was still thinking.

"And a man who came to visit Faisal on his sickbed gave us a gift of money . . ." The more she thought, the more she was able to recall gifts of money and goods from various people, as well as friends who showed true sorrow for her loss and sympathy toward her family. Perhaps God actually was taking care of them.

"Wonderful! Don't you see, Shareen? God is already answering your prayers. While the whole world is spinning in space and leaders of countries are having their wars and everything, God sees you, right here in your house. He knows who you are and He hears you and answers your prayers. He's proven that He cares about you by blessing you and doing good to you, just like you asked Him to."

She smiled for the first time in weeks. Could this Christian doctrine be right? Could it be true that the God of the universe actually cares about individual people personally?

She smiled for the first time in weeks. Could it be true that the God of the universe actually cares about individual people personally?

Arriving home that night, I told Mike everything. We agreed that we could hardly call ourselves Shareen and Faisal's friends if we didn't do something to help. Doling out some grocery money, Mike instructed me to buy what they needed. The plan was to go to the market very early so the supplies could be discreetly left within their walls before they woke up. It would be better if no one knew who it was from.

The next morning I purchased the items and took them to Shareen's. Joy bubbled up in my heart as I lined up sacks of rice and flour, food and household supplies. Suddenly the door of the house opened and one of Shareen's sons came out. We were both surprised to see each other. What was he doing up so early? What was I doing there at all?

"Mom, Reema's here!" he announced over his shoulder.

Coming into the yard, Shareen took one look at the pile of goods and clapped her hands against her cheeks. Her mouth dropped open. Waving her hands in the air, she began shouting something I couldn't understand. I was a bit embarrassed by all the commotion, unaware of the real reason for my friend's ecstatic display of happiness.

Absolutely glowing with wonder, she explained. "Early this morning I was sleeping and had a dream. It was so real that I thought I was awake. In the dream, I was putting sacks full of food onto my bare kitchen shelves, and I felt so happy! But when I woke up and realized it was just a dream,

and that we still had nothing, I began to cry again. That's
when I remembered what we were talking about last night.
So I prayed and asked God to give us sacks for our kitchen
shelves. Like in the dream. Just as I finished praying I heard
my son calling me from out here. And when I came out,
there you were with the sacks!"

In an instant I was just as overwhelmed with joy as Shareen,
and the two of us stood there in the yard shouting praises to
God together. It was obvious to both of us that I could not
have possibly known she would have that particular dream or
pray that particular prayer on this particular day. Rather "it is
God who works in you both to will and to do for His good
pleasure" (Philippians 2:13) for "we are God's fellow workers"
(1 Corinthians 3:9). Rejoicing together, we knew that God
was making Himself known to Shareen and her family,
personally.

Mike needed a key one day and headed off to see our building attendant. A young man in his twenties, Ibrahiim was
a likable character. When the neighborhood kids came
out in the street to play, he stopped working to sit down
and watch over them. At least, we assumed he'd stopped
working. Once a week he would wash the stairwell inside
our building by standing on the topmost step with a hose

in his hand and letting the water run down all three stories, hopefully carrying away part of the accumulated debris. Other than that, we really didn't know what he did to earn his pay. Nevertheless, with our balcony view of the street below, we came to appreciate Ibrahiim's dealings with the children. He was quick to intervene in any bullying, warn them if a car was coming, or take charge when the playing got out of hand.

Another thing we liked about Ibrahiim was how he took care of his widowed mother, Umm Ibrahiim. They shared a tiny room in the basement, which he was afforded as part of his salary, and seemed thankful to have it. Life had been very hard for them, and the suffering they had shared made them even dearer to one another. If Umm Ibrahiim overheard her son talking inappropriately to Mike about women, alcohol, or some other subject, she'd reprimand him lovingly in front of us. In full support of Mike's fatherly admonitions against such behaviors, she'd chime right in, "You tell him, Mr. Mike! Tell my son that's not the way for good men to talk. He's been listening to those young men and their foolishness. If his father were here, he would tell him. You tell him, Mr. Mike!"

And Mike did. Ibrahiim seemed to like that. Though the moral exhortations were well received, neither Ibrahiim nor his mother showed any interest at all in spiritual things. As for us, we barely even mentioned them in our prayers, though we wrestled long and hard on behalf of others we knew, those with whom we were actively sharing the Gospel. After all, we thought, shouldn't we focus our prayers and invest our efforts where we could clearly see God at work? It just didn't seem like God was doing anything in the lives of our building attendant or his mother. That is, until the day Mike went to borrow the key.

"Here it is." Ibrahiim put the key into Mike's hand. "Just bring it back later."

"I will. Thanks."

"Would you like to come in for a cup of tea?" After all, who does business in Arabia without at least a cup of tea?

"Sure, thanks." Mike went in and made himself comfortable.

Handing his guest a steaming cup, Ibrahiim sat down and quietly announced, "I had a dream."

The statement in itself seemed like no big deal. Completely unaware of the direction their conversation was about to take, Mike asked the obvious question, "What was your dream?"

✛

Ibrahiim sat down and quietly announced, "I had a dream."

✛

"Well, one night I was sleeping," the young man began. "I was sleeping but I heard someone calling my name. *Ibrahiim. Ibrahiim.* So I sat up and looked, and there at the foot of my bed was this . . . this man. But he was like nothing I've ever seen before.

He wasn't standing on the ground; he was somehow above it. And he was wearing brilliant clothes of amazing white-ness, with a band of shining gold around his waist and across his chest. His hair and beard were dazzling white-gold. And there was *light* . . . coming from his face . . ."

Mike's attention was riveted. The tea forgotten, he hung on every word as Ibrahiim continued the story.

"Then he stretched out his hand toward me." In Arab culture, a person of high rank or position allows himself to be kissed on the back of the hand, the forehead, or shoulder by those wishing to honor him and show their respect. "I got up to kiss it, but he pulled it back and said, 'Pray to your God.' Then, he vanished."

Mike's mind was racing but he remained outwardly calm, "So did you 'pray to your God'?"

"No." The reply sounded like a guilty confession. "I just couldn't. I've tried many times, but something inside just keeps me from doing it."

"Who was it?"

Ibrahiim's immediate response was to say "Muhammad," yet Mike sensed that he was unconvinced.

"And how do you know it was Muhammad?"

"I told the dream to a *mutawwa*, and he said it was Muhammad. That was six years ago. You're the first person I've told since."

Six years! He'd been waiting to know who really appeared to him for *six years*? Thankful that Ibrahiim hadn't been comfortable praying to the god indicated by the *mutawwa*'s opinion, Mike excused himself to run upstairs for a minute. Grabbing a Bible from our flat, he returned to the basement apartment and opened it to Revelation 1. Pointing to verses 12 through 18 in the Arabic text, he asked Ibrahiim to read.

As the young man read the passage, his eyes grew as big as saucers. He looked up at Mike for a moment and then read it again. By the third time, his face had completely fallen, and he looked pale. Holding the Bible in one hand, he put a trembling finger on the page.

"Who wrote this? What book is this? *This* is who I saw!"

"Ibrahiim, Muhammad is dead. You saw the Lord Jesus Christ."

Amazingly, Ibrahiim had never heard of the Bible. Only after considerable prompting from Mike could he recollect that the Quran mentioned something about another Book. It didn't matter. He wanted it. He wanted to devour this Book that so vividly described the One he had seen. Mike gave him the Bible, and for the next four days, Ibrahiim did not sleep. He just read and thought, and read and thought, all day and all night. He completed the entire New Testament in a week. After that he understood just who Jesus the Messiah really was—and what he himself had to do. Now he was counting the cost.

Clearly, Ibrahiim was completely unaware that many, many Muslims from all over the globe had at one time faced the decision he was now facing and had left Islam to follow Christ. Since he had grown up in a Muslim country, his exposure to world news excluded such "anti-Islamic" tidbits. Naturally, he had accepted the things that constituted "common knowledge" in his culture, just as we do in ours. In his case, that included the "fact" that no Muslim in history had ever converted to another religion.

He believed that he was completely unique in his struggle and supremely alone— the very first Muslim to deny his religion.

He believed that he was completely unique in his struggle and supremely alone—the very first Muslim to deny his religion. Although untrue, the fact that he believed this only added to the magnitude of the already enormous decision before him. To him it was a choice between Jesus and, literally, his whole world.

The empathy of his American neighbors did little to help Ibrahiim. Assuming Mike and I to be ignorant regarding the seriousness of his situation, he confided to me one day, "Mrs. Mike, you don't know what it means. You don't know what it means if I believe what the Bible says about Jesus.

I'm a Muslim. Muslims cannot become Christians. If I make this decision, it means my life. They will take my life."

Of course it was true that our friend had every earthly reason to fear. When I tried to hearten him with stories of other Muslims who had come to know the Lord, he seemed to think I was speaking from misguided hearsay. Unable to give him names or introduce him to a convert for the sake of their security, my words appeared empty indeed. How I wished a Muslim-background believer would come alongside our young friend and encourage him with his own testimony of salvation. But no one did. Understandably, the "comforting" of a foreigner who'd been born in freedom was no comfort at all. And so Ibrahiim actually was all alone, albeit unnecessarily, in his struggle.

One morning, while Mike was dropping off the kids at school, our apartment intercom buzzed. It had been about ten days since Ibrahiim shared his dream and began reading the Bible. His voice now crackled over the ancient wires connecting us. "Mrs. Mike, when Mr. Mike gets home, can you ask him to come and see me? I'm ready to pray."

Hallelujah!

That day saw the long-overdue fulfillment of a heavenly command. Ibrahiim "prayed to his God." In true, honorable Arab form, he'd bathed and put on fresh clothes and cologne out of respect for the occasion. Looking at Mike, he instructed, "A few words at a time. I will repeat after you. And make sure you get in the part about forgiveness of sin."

The glory filling his newly cleansed heart shone through his face.

In the next moment, Ibrahiim became a child of God through faith in the Lord Jesus Christ.

He was radiant. The glory filling his newly cleansed heart shone through his face. I couldn't help but ask how he felt. Smiling broadly, glowing with new life and freedom, he said, "The fear is gone! I'm not afraid anymore. Now if they kill me," he pointed upward, " I know where I'll go!"

The very next thing he wanted to do was to share a picture Bible with his mother. She, too, needed to meet the glorious Savior he now knew.

✦ ✦ ✦

Until recently, the majority of Muslims who became Christians did so in part because of a dream or a vision. Although we can't speak for others, Mike and I can say that our first convert, first baptism, and first disciple—all three men— were each influenced by a dream or vision they'd had. Interestingly, the same vision that Ibrahiim related in the story above has been described by other Muslims as well. But Muslims aren't the only people having dreams and visions.

At a large conference on ministry to Muslims, held in the United States, I was approached on several occasions between sessions by different women who had been burdened to pray specifically for the Arab Muslim World. Each one of them had had an unusual experience during a particular season of prayer.

Cynthia, a believer since childhood, had grown up in the Church and was heavily involved in her local Body. She was also a homeschooling mom with five children. With all that going on, it was a wonder she had the energy to pray for people so remote and distant from her life. Yet she'd been doing it for three years! Excitedly, she told me that during one of her prayer times she'd "seen" something. It was a vision of the globe, turning slowly on its axis. Her view was zooming in on a specific region, the Arabian Peninsula. Then, a specific country, and then a specific city, and then—*crack!* The map split open and light was pouring out of the crack. She felt that God was showing her a spiritual breakthrough taking place in the very land she was interceding for. Amazingly, two other women at the conference reported a similar experience.

She felt that God was showing her a spiritual breakthrough taking place in the very land she was interceding for.

During one of the conference lunches, I happened to

sit next to Phyllis, an exuberant believer and ardent prayer warrior. She was telling the people at our table about a strange experience she'd had just recently. While wrestling in prayer for the ethnic ministries that her inner-city church was pioneering, the Holy Spirit seemed to interrupt her and say, *Pray for Almakaan.* Her first thought was, *Who or what is Almakaan?* Although she didn't know what it was, she obediently prayed. Later, her pastor approached her and gave her tickets to the conference we were now at. Thinking the two might be connected, she'd been asking everyone, "Do you know *Almakaan? Al Makaan? Alma Kaan?*"

I was stunned. Momentarily speechless, I had to push my words out. "I know what *Almakaan* is."

Phyllis's eyes locked on mine. "You *know?* What is it?"

"*Almakaan* is a city. It's located in the Arab Muslim country where I live, and three women at this conference just told me they've had a vision of a major spiritual breakthrough there."

If God is burdening people that specifically to pray for His work, then surely He is working. He is answering those prayers!

✢

Now you are the body of Christ,
and members individually.

1 CORINTHIANS 12:27

CHAPTER 8

It Takes a Body

Back in the days when we were living in the apartment, the time came for Mike to make a ministry trip out of the country, leaving me and the kids home alone. Brief separations had been an accepted part of life, and neither he nor I thought anything much of it. It turned out to be two of the longest weeks of my life.

During the day life went on as usual, but every night there was trouble. Both of the kids were having a big problem with a "scary feeling" in their room, even though they shared the same bedroom and were less than six feet away from each other. Each night, two-year-old Lydia seemed to develop a sudden high fever and other alarming symptoms of illness, all of which disappeared in the morning. Once I took her into bed with me to keep an eye on her and she appeared to be hallucinating, looking at something in the air and grasping at it with her fingers. Then she got out of bed, lay down on the floor, and pushed herself in circles with her legs. There were other weird goings-on, and our home began to feel like a dark place.

On the phone with Mike, I tried to explain what we were going through, and he prayed for us. I prayed for us. The kids prayed for us. We prayed for each other. And did I mention we prayed? Yet nothing changed. I thought I might lose my sanity if this spiritual oppression didn't let up. Wasn't God stronger than Satan? Of course He was—so why didn't He answer our prayers?

We'd had reason to ask these kinds of questions many times in the past, too, and had discovered at least one of the answers. It seemed to be God's way of reminding us how dependent we are on other Christians. You know what I'm talking about. God uses someone's gifts, abilities, personality, life experience, background, or training to benefit you one day, and He uses yours to benefit someone else the next. God intentionally designed it so that we each need what the others have to offer. Growing weary in our time of trouble reminded us again—we needed the Body of Christ!

We knew several expat believers, yet I felt so isolated. The few Christians I'd felt comfortable revealing our troubles to had looked at me strangely, not quite knowing what to make of such experiences. I got the impression that sharing the need had made them question my spirituality, and I wasn't up to defending myself. I needed someone who knew what to do to come and do it. But who?

Late one afternoon, as the time was approaching for the sunset "call to prayer" from local mosques, our doorbell rang. Opening the door, I was shocked to see three perky, middle-aged American church ladies smiling happily at me. They looked their Sunday best, dressed in brightly colored clothing with matching accessories. Perfectly coiffed hair and attractive makeup enhanced the radiant glow of their bright faces. How starkly they stood out against the drab brown backdrop of our town, where everything was covered with a conspicuous coat of desert dust and where colorless, faceless, black-robed figures milled about the streets.

Unable to believe my eyes, I racked my brain. **Who can they possibly be? And how did they find us?**

Unable to believe my eyes, I racked my brain. *Who can they possibly be? And how did they find us?* We didn't even have a writable address here in our maze of nameless, numberless streets! I wondered if they were angels.

They studied me for a moment. A compassionate look came over one woman's face, and her voice gently broke through my stunned silence.

"Are you okay?"

Instantly the four of us "connected"—they were believers! Explaining that I was not okay, I described our plight. It turned out they had just come from the States and were searching for a friend, who turned out to be the student who had just moved in upstairs. Accidentally, they had knocked on the wrong door. Realizing that the mistake was God's intended way of bringing them to my family's aid, they went right to work. I believe the Holy Spirit led them as those women prayed through every room of our house. They claimed Scripture, forbade evil, and called down blessing in Jesus' name. When they left, I was still crying tears of gratitude and relief.

With that, the night troubles were over. God had faithfully provided for our family even when we felt the most isolated and powerless. Through other believers, He revived us and brought refreshment and light back into our home. We believe our heavenly Father escorted those sisters straight from their homes in the United States to our door, specifically to intercede on our behalf. Obviously we were blessed by them, but they were also blessed to be the answer to our prayers. Giver and receiver were built up and God was glorified. What a sense of connectedness and unity comes from the fact that without even knowing each other, we can be there for each other, guided by our mutual Father.

Incidents like these, where God deliberately chooses to work in a seemingly implausible way and through sources outside of ourselves, remind us that our Christian faith is based on solid reality. My family and I thrill to see the spiritual truths that we walk in by faith manifest themselves in our flesh-and-blood life here on earth. Don't you? I think God delights in doing it too! How blessed each of us is to be part of His Church. We are not merely isolated individuals with a common religious label; we truly are children of God! We're part of a Kingdom so real and so great that it's not only international, or global, or universal; it's eternal! *Thank God* for the Body of Christ!

It was a very busy day at the sheikha's public *majlis*. Many people filled the sitting areas, waiting for the privilege of greeting this female member of Big Town's most powerful family. A perfectly groomed and impeccably dressed aide was overseeing the hospitality as servants scurried in and out with trays of refreshments. I remembered the aide from past visits because of her calm yet commanding demeanor, the serene look of confidence she seemed to have, and her white socks. For some reason I'd noticed she always wore white socks.

Traffic inside the room being rather heavy, she stepped

forward and took a tray from one of her charges and began
distributing its contents. The servant hurried back to the
kitchen for a replacement, while White Socks worked her
way through a group of chatting guests. She was heading my
way. Something about her appearance made me think she
was probably strict about her religion and might be well-
educated in the Quran. When she was close enough, I tried
to start a conversation with her.

"Peace be upon you," I offered with a friendly smile.

"And upon you," she replied mechanically.

Cheered by the response, I continued, "You're certainly
very busy with so many visitors today. If you have a moment
sometime I'd like to ask you a question."

White Socks did not return the cheer. Her voice was as
crisp as her well-starched, precisely ironed clothing. "I have
time. What is your question?"

"Well, I've been reading a little of the Quran and came
across something that confuses me. When I asked my
Muslim friends about it, none of them could explain it."

Her interest seemed slightly perked. "You've been reading
the Quran?"

"Well, just a bit. I'm no scholar about this kind of
thing, of course, but I happened to notice two places in
the Quran where Muslims are told to read and believe the
Bible because it was sent down from God in Truth and His

words can't be changed. Yet, all my
friends and neighbors say they're not
supposed to read the Bible because it's
corrupted and full of errors. So I guess
what I'm wondering is: Where do
Islamic teachers get this doctrine—
which seems to be the exact opposite
of what the Quran says—and why do
so many sincere Muslims accept it?
I mean, well, it doesn't seem to make
sense." Such thought-provoking ques-

"*Where do Islamic
teachers get this
doctrine—which
seems to be the
exact opposite of
what the Quran
says—and why do so
many sincere
Muslims accept it?*"

tions, asked in a genuine and kind manner, often lead to
further discussion or even the opportunity to offer a Bible.

With no sign of emotion whatsoever, White Socks
excused herself. A moment later she returned and asked me
to write down the verses I was talking about, Suras 4:136
and 6:114-115. Holding the piece of paper up like key evidence at a trial, she informed me that it would be taken to
the sheikha herself for an answer. I got the feeling that White
Socks did not like me or my question. Perhaps she hoped to
rouse her mistress, and thus her mistress's family, against me.
When it was finally my turn to greet the sheikha, I wondered
what would happen next. Certainly this family had it in their
power to do whatever they pleased. Rulers were known to
act on whims or out of passion, not being bound to any due

processes of law. By the grace of God, the sheikha's response was both detached and good-humored. Busy with more important things, and recognizing that the question was a religious one, she generously arranged to send a *mutawwa* directly to our home to address the matter in person!

On the one hand Mike and I were thrilled at such an amazing opportunity. On the other hand, we were nervous about the suddenly serious potential consequences. Given who was sending him, this *mutawwa* was probably a high-level person with clout. Perhaps he was the family's personal religious consultant, or maybe he was from the Ministry of Islamic Affairs. Whoever he was, what he reported back to the sheikha could have major repercussions—and not only for us. What about other Christians living here? We felt like we were in way over our heads. There was only one thing to do: we contacted other believers and asked them to pray.

The *mutawwa* called in the morning to let us know that he planned to arrive at the normal evening visiting hour and, being too busy himself, had his interpreter get directions. A number of the believers we'd notified had passed on our prayer request, so the word had spread. Many of those who got the message belonged to small groups that met for mutual encouragement, support, and prayer. It just "so happened" that this particular day of the week was when a lot of them had their meetings. As a result, there were actually entire teams of Christians praying for the *mutawwa*'s visit while it was happening. Clearly, this was God's timing. Later, we'd all be amazed to learn what an orchestration of the Body of Christ actually took place as other believers interceded on our behalf.

When the Church eventually gathered for fellowship, our brothers and sisters were as eager to hear how the rendezvous had gone as we were to tell them. One by one, both individuals and groups who had been in various locations that night expressed how they'd felt led to pray in very specific ways, sometimes in the very same words. The more we listened to them, the more clearly we saw the unity of their inspired prayers. Some reported that they were actually "interrupted" by the Holy Spirit more than once during the course of their meeting and moved to pray some more. A few had felt as if their prayers were being answered even as they were praying. Apparently, they were. What the intercessors asked for is what happened at our house . . .

A few had felt as if their prayers were being answered even as they were praying. Apparently, they were.

"Lord, we ask You that all Islamic rhetoric would be confounded. Cause the mutawwa *and his interpreter to forget their vain arguments and actually listen. Let them hear Truth."*

They did! Several times, both the *mutawwa* and his well-trained interpreter had tried to get the conversation off on to one of those prepackaged tangents but completely lost their train of thought. As their words trailed off, we could see the mental struggle on their faces. They just couldn't remember what they were talking about. The Islamic rhetoric was confounded. They forgot their vain arguments. And they wound up listening instead. Really listening.

There was peace in the room as our main guest considered one point silently for several minutes. Meanwhile, the interpreter was peering closely at a passage he'd just read and reread several times.

"Oh God, please lift the veil from their understanding . . ."

Slowly, the interpreter lifted his eyeglasses and removed them from his face. Leaning forward, with his eyes still fixed on the text, he read it again.

". . . and give them revelation."

"I see it!" he shouted. "*I see it!*" Excitedly, he looked around at each of us. A revelation had dawned upon him. Suddenly, he realized what our question meant, why it had to be answered, and how significant the ramifications might be. This was an issue at the very crux of his Islamic faith. Although he'd read the Quran numerous times, he had never grasped the dilemma he now saw so clearly. As the open book lay before him, he turned a suspicious eye on his friend.

His brow furrowed as he scowled, "Why *do* you say the Bible has been changed?"

The hint of accusation had abruptly put our *mutawwa* on the spot. Certainly, both men had experienced a major challenge to their faith this evening, and there was no need to add insult to injury. We wanted to continue—and build— our relationship with them if they were willing. For that reason, Mike and I were eager to help the *mutawwa* save face with his friend. Gladly, we accepted his next proposal.

Outwardly unruffled, he passed over the accusation as if he hadn't heard it. Instead, he fixed his gaze on Mike and me. "I will do something for you," he offered in a benevolent manner. "Write this concern of yours here on my paper. I am going to take it home and consider it, and then we will come back and talk to you again."

This apparently temperate and open-minded response reclaimed some of his companion's respect. "Excellent," the interpreter smiled. Reassured of the *mutawwa*'s integrity and scholarly objectivity, he added, "I want to understand this for myself. After all, we all want the truth."

A few days later we received a phone call from a government official. "I understand my friend the *mutawwa* visited you in regard to a question concerning the Quran. I think I can answer it better than he. Is it possible for us to meet this week to discuss the matter?" Although the *mutawwa* never did return with an answer, he apparently shared the question with other Muslims. How far did that question travel, and to whom? What further affect has it had? Only the Head who moves the Body knows.

✝

*And I, brethren,
when I came to you,
did not come with
excellence of speech or of
wisdom declaring to you
the testimony of God. . . .
I was with you in weakness,
in fear, and in much
trembling. And my speech
and my preaching were
not with persuasive words
of human wisdom, but in
demonstration of the
Spirit and of power,
that your faith should
not be in the wisdom
of men but in the
power of God.*

PAUL THE APOSTLE,

1 CORINTHIANS 2:1, 3-5

CHAPTER 9

Mercy Drops

You may have heard that in 2004 the film *The Passion of the Christ* set box-office records in several Arab countries. These are Muslim countries. Tickets were in such demand that some cineplexes had several theaters showing the film at once. In one Arab state, it played one hundred times a day to packed-out audiences. Local papers did news stories on it and even carried front-page ads for it. The interest originally seemed to stem from the fact that it was an American film rumored to be anti-Semitic. Since the Middle East generally perceives the United States and Israel as cohorts, many were eager to watch it. What they saw once they were in their seats, however, was something very different than expected. How like God to use even human conflict and ill will to spread His grace and "goodwill toward men." Reports came in from both Levantine and Gulf nations that Arab Muslims were being moved by the Gospel of our Lord Jesus Christ. Christians in the crowd saw tears on Muslim cheeks as they watched the Savior of the world forgive His mocking enemies from the cross. Sobered audiences sat in silence long after the film had ended and filed quietly out afterward.

Good news is popping up all over, and at times in very unexpected places. In December 2001, the influential and widely viewed Arab news agency Al Jazeera did a live interview with Sheikh Ahmad al Qataani to report on the problem of large numbers of Muslims converting to Christianity in the African nations. Al Qataani, a Saudi Arabian Sunni leader, estimated 6 million Muslims turning to Christ per year! Although we cannot verify his numbers, the fact that Islamic leaders admit Muslims are leaving the faith is new history. In the past, propaganda has claimed that no Muslim has ever left Islam because its followers are so satisfied they feel no need for anything else. Even if al Qataani's statistics were inflated to incite alarm and rally Muslims to stem the tide, that in itself would

Imagine how encouraging it must be to a Muslim seeker or secret believer to hear through Islamic sources that, not only are they not alone in their spiritual journey, they are part of a movement.

mean there is a tide to stem. Either way it's more good news. Imagine how encouraging it must be to a Muslim seeker or secret believer to hear through Islamic sources that, not only are they not alone in their spiritual journey, they are part of a movement.

And the movement is growing. Muslim-background believers (MBBs) are becoming involved in reaching their own people with the Gospel. They pray. They personally witness. They share testimonies. They write literature. They help produce outreach media. You can hear them share their testimonies on YouTube or meet with them in chat rooms.

MBBs staff the chat room and phone lines for Father Zakaria Botros's hugely successful evangelistic satellite TV show. It is estimated that perhaps 50 million Muslims each day tune in to this ninety-minute Arabic program, which has been translated into other languages and broadcast around the world. So many Muslims have come to Christ through this Egyptian minister's zealous teaching and preaching that he's been declared Islam's "public enemy number one" by the Arabic press. Al Qaeda has even put a price on his head. Our family first heard about him through Arab friends who told us that Muslims hate him but can't resist turning on his show to see what he's going to say next.

But these are just mercy drops hitting the shore. A tidal wave is coming. Thousands of copies of the Arabic Bible

are being downloaded from the Internet every month. The
Web is abuzz with hits to both Arabic and English sites
geared to reaching Muslims. The inquiries and response
by Muslims to Arab Christian programming on both radio
and TV have become more than some ministries can even
handle. Gospel mini-movies are being passed along mobile
phones, iPods, BlackBerries, and Bluetooth devices. Besides
technology, there is old-fashioned one-on-one dialogue.
Arabs who patronize popular vacation spots in non-Islamic
countries acquire Bibles, Gospel literature, and media
firsthand from Christian workers there. Right at home on
Arabian soil, seekers and MBBs meet with Christian friends
to study the Bible and talk out their beliefs. We've heard
of MBBs meeting in cars or driving out into the desert to
fellowship, sing, and worship because there is no place else
that's safe for them to meet. A few years ago, MBBs from
two Arab countries held their own conference, praying and
discussing how to reach their nations for Christ.

The song of joy among missionaries these days is that
more Muslims have come to Christ in the past three decades
than in the last fourteen centuries! So what's different? Why
now? Of course it goes without saying that the timing for
this harvest is according to God's sovereign plan. And clearly
prayer is a major part of that plan. In recent decades there
has been record-setting prayer and petition, even agonized

intercession, made by the saints on behalf of the Muslim World. One great example of this is a story I heard from Nik Ripken.

The song of joy among missionaries these days is that more Muslims have come to Christ in the past three decades than in the last fourteen centuries!

Nik Ripken, veteran missionary and noted researcher of the persecuted church, was in China a number of years ago to conduct interviews at a gathering of over 150 indigenous church leaders. These men and women were representatives of a church-planting movement numbering about 10 million Chinese believers. At the end of one exhausting day of asking questions, listening, and asking more questions, Nik was ready to turn in. His new brothers and sisters, however, had some questions of their own to ask.

Having little knowledge of what God was doing elsewhere in the world, they wanted to know if there were Christians in places other than China. (What a telling moment.) Needless to say, they were thrilled when they heard the answer! Next they wanted to know if other believers were suffering persecution like them. Nik chose to tell them stories of Muslim converts from two different Arab countries who had suffered greatly for their witness of the Lord Jesus Christ. Strangely, his Chinese audience did not appear to respond at all to what he shared. *Perhaps,* Nik thought, *they are so used to suffering that such stories do not move them anymore.* After all, in China it is expected that a follower of Christ will be kicked out of his family and probably spend at least three years in jail. No one is even allowed to serve in Church leadership until they've spent some time in prison for their faith. Still, the response (or lack of it) bothered Nik, and he dragged himself off to bed deeply discouraged.

About 6 a.m., Nik awoke to the sounds of crying and shouting. Was it a raid? Had the Chinese police found their gathering place? Rushing outside, he found what seemed to be mass hysteria. It appeared that all of the more than 150 conference participants were on the ground. Some were sitting; others were kneeling or lying prostrate. Still others seemed to be beating themselves in some sort of anguish. Unable to understand the language, Nik sought an interpreter to tell him what was going on. Moving briskly through the crowd, he thought he could hear three words that he did recognize being repeated over and over. The words were *Muslim* and the names of the two countries he had told them about the night before. They were praying. No, they were pouring out their souls to God in intercession for Muslims whose existence they'd only learned about a few hours ago. That day, those leaders made a commitment to share this news with their churches and to get up one hour earlier each day in order to intercede at the throne of grace "until God does something."

If "the effective, fervent prayer of a righteous man avails much" (James 5:16), what happens when that many believers pray?

A year later, Nik was back in one of the countries he had told his Chinese friends about. The Christians there had big news. After centuries of stone-wall resistance to the Gospel, something had broken in the spiritual realm. Instead of resistance, or even tolerance, Muslims were actually seeking Truth—a staggering change from just one year to the next!

And, of course, it is not only the Chinese who pray. Believers across the planet are involved. Window International Network (WIN) claims to have helped some 40 million Christian believers in 120 countries pray through the 10/40 Window, where the world's most unreached people live. Other ministries, such as the Arabian Peninsula Partnership (APP), sharpen their prayer focus even more specifically onto the region of the world where Islam was birthed. Praying Through the Arabian Peninsula (PTAP) is devoted solely to informing and equipping saints around the world to pray for the seven Muslim nations that make up the AP: Saudi Arabia, Kuwait, Qatar, Bahrain, United Arab Emirates, Oman, and Yemen. Their weekly e-letter brings fresh prayer requests, answers to prayer, and brief testimonies from workers on the ground. It is estimated that well over a million people are finding fuel for their intercession, in two dozen languages, through PTAP and its network.

Admittedly, this book you hold in your hand reveals only a smattering of what's happening. God is using multitudes of Christians, all sorts of people, in incalculable ways through innumerable venues to shine the light of His love on the face of Islam. It's the Body of Christ reaching out in every which way to the Community (*Umma*) of Islam. Here "on the ground" we are seeing the results of those cumulative efforts, and we wanted you to know it.

Thank you for doing your part in spreading the knowledge of His glory throughout the earth. We join our voices with yours in praising the Lord of the Harvest, giving "thanks to the LORD for His goodness, and for His wonderful works to the children of men!" (Psalm 107:31).

To God be the glory!

More Information

English language sites for Christians, with links to other languages

www.pray-ap.info (Praying Through the Arabian Peninsula)

www.apinfo.eu (Arabian Peninsula Partnership Europe)

www.30-days.net (Prayer site)

www.morethandreams.org (Personal stories of believers from Muslim backgrounds)

www.resource-international.info (Site listing Arabic resources for outreach)

www.answering-islam.org (FAQs answered)

www.engagingislam.org (Information on training seminars for evangelism and discipleship)

Arabic sites for interested Muslims and believers from Muslim backgrounds

www.arabicbible.com (Arabic Bible in different formats)

www.dreamsandvisions.com (Personal stories of believers from Muslim backgrounds)

www.islameyat.com (Arabic audio and video teaching; *Daring Questions* program)

www.arabicprograms.org (TWR audio site in Arabic)

www.inarabic.org (Arabic discipleship site)

www.borjalmaarifa.org (Discipling new believers from a Muslim background through e-learning)

www.takwin-masihi.org (PALM discipleship materials)

Online Discussion
guide

TₐKE *your* TYNDALE READING
EXPERIENCE *to the* NEXT LEVEL

A FREE discussion guide for this book
is available at bookclubhub.net, perfect
for sparking conversations in your book
group or for digging deeper into the text
on your own.

www.bookclubhub.net

*You'll also find free discussion guides for
other Tyndale books, e-newsletters, e-mail
devotionals, virtual book tours, and more!*